THE STRUGGLE

I dedicate this book to the
three women in my life:
Jane, Antje and Amy.

THE STRUGGLE

The Battle between Flesh and Spirit

Hartmut Kopsch

Terra Nova Publications Ltd.
Bristol

First published in 1998
Reprinted 2000

The publishers acknowledge with appreciation financial assistance toward the publication of this book, granted by The Drummond Trust, 3 Pitt Terrace, Stirling.

The cover illustration is from a painting by Frog Orr-Ewing

ISBN 1 901949 01 X

Published in Great Britain by Terra Nova Publications Ltd.
Orders and enquiries: PO Box 2400 Bradford on Avon BA15 2YN
Registered Office (not for trade): 21 St.Thomas Street, Bristol BS1 6JS

Typeset by Ex Libris Press, Bradford-on-Avon, Wiltshire
Printed and bound in Great Britain by The Cromwell Press, White Horse Business Park, Trowbridge, Wiltshire BA14 0XB

CONTENTS

ACKNOWLEDGEMENTS

I would like to make the following acknowledgements:

To my son-in-law Francis Orr-Ewing for providing the cover illustration which is from a silk painting he presented to my daughter, Amy, on their wedding day. It depicts his hopes for their lives together, namely placing themselves, with their strengths and weaknesses, at the foot of the cross.

To the people of St. Christopher's, Birmingham, because I did most of the work on this book while I was their Vicar.

To Peter and Jane Byron Davies for their encouragement and help in publishing this book.

Hartmut Kopsch

Chapter One

The Flesh and the Spirit

Some years ago, during a particularly difficult period in my life, God showed me a vision of a necklace around my neck, that was squeezing the life out of me. So strong was the pressure from this squeezing that I tried with both hands, while fully conscious, to tear the necklace from my neck. I was shown in the vision that the necklace represented the flesh which was determined to dominate my life and put out the life of the Spirit.[1] God further revealed to me that there were five beads on this necklace, and that each bead represented one manifestation of the flesh. This crisis in my life was followed by a process of being broken from a strongly entrenched self-reliance.

The first bead God showed me was jealousy. I remember distinctly arguing with God for two days and insisting that whatever other feelings I had, jealousy was not one of them. Then the Lord revealed to me past relationships and situations in which I had had feelings of jealousy, and how such feelings would suddenly surface with little provocation. Someone would be warmly praised in my presence and my peace would be shattered. These feelings were especially strong where the praise for another was in an area of life close to my heart, such as my gifts, achievements or desires for success in personal or professional life; or where blessings, favour or success came to others in ways that I coveted. Such words would bother me in my inmost being, robbing me of peace. The Lord showed many such instances, and I capitulated. 'Yes, Lord. You are right. I am jealous and it is amazing that I have never seen it as a problem in myself that needs to be sorted out.' I repented of all my past jealous feelings and thoughts, and then the Lord showed me the spiritual opposite to jealousy—compassion. I remember being surprised, but I did not argue. The other four beads, with their spiritual opposites, were also revealed, as the meaning of the vision unfolded. They were: envy and covetousness in place of love; pride opposed to humility; fear rather than faith, and loudmouthedness as opposed to gentleness.

As I thought about all these manifestations of the flesh in my life and their positive spiritual opposites, I turned to the Word of God to gain understanding of the way the flesh works and how to resist its urges. This developed into a study of the struggle between the flesh and the Spirit, each bead of the necklace providing a basis from which to start. I realise that the particular beads of my necklace are personal to me. Others might be aware of different 'strongholds' or besetting sins that God would have them tackle, such as unforgiveness, resentment or lust. Whatever the particular 'beads' might be, the principles for victory are the same.

When we become aware of any sin, our starting point is the cross, and the awareness that Jesus suffered there for our precise sin—enabling us to be wonderfully forgiven and cleansed, and empowered to resist future temptations. As we bring ourselves, our burdens and sins, to the cross in repentance, the Holy Spirit empowers us to live differently. Jesus died to free us from all the accumulated baggage we have gathered and, when we turn to him, wants us to enjoy life 'in abundance' and an unhindered relationship with him. But we are often not living like this much of the time.

As the meaning of the necklace unfolded and I came to grips with each bead, I was overwhelmed by the tremendous peace of knowing the total forgiveness of God in every area of failure, and the joy of walking with Him in intimacy. At my conversion, I had experienced an overpowering sense of the love of God for me. Somehow, much of this had evaporated over the years. A regained consciousness of the wonder of God's love for me became a significant factor in the dynamics of living in the Spirit. When we have the revelation of the greatness of God's love for us, and when we meditate on that love, it helps us to live in the Spirit so that the flesh is defeated. Paul puts it like this:

> ...that you, being rooted and established in love, may have power, together with all the saints, to grasp how wide and long and high and deep is the love of Christ, and to know this love that surpasses knowledge—that you may be filled to the measure of all the fulness of God.
>
> *Ephesians 3:17b-19*

When we are able to take in the extent and intensity of Christ's love for us, our inner being is so strengthened by the Spirit that any pressures from the flesh are more easily resisted. In my study of scripture, I was often engaged with episodes in the Old Testament. It occurred to me that the very struggle between the flesh and the Spirit which every

Christian faces might find parallels there. All the important Christian doctrines are to be found in the Old Testament, at least in the sense that in it those doctrines are foreshadowed. For example, the doctrine of redemption is to be seen clearly in the book of Exodus. In the struggle between Israel and the Amalekites, which is the theme of the second chapter of this book, we see a foreshadowing of the Christian's struggle against the flesh.

When defining 'the flesh', it is helpful to distinguish between the Greek and Christian concepts. The Greeks saw the body as intrinsically evil, the noble soul needing to be delivered from it. The dualistic Greek view of soul against body, good against evil, has a superficial parallel with the Biblical distinction between the flesh and the Spirit but, in essence, is very different. Paul's view of mankind is tripartite. We are body (the outward material shell with life visible), soul (inner life, embracing mind, emotions and will), and spirit (the innermost 'secret' dimension through which we are able to commune with God).[2] The flesh comprises the soul and the body acting together independently of God. It is our nature—spoiled, not only by our own sin, but also by our parents' sins, and dominated by self, with its passions and desires. The Spirit is the Holy Spirit, who dwells in every believer. The struggle between the flesh and the Spirit is the struggle of every Christian. It begins at conversion, as a result of the rebellion by the flesh against losing its total control over the convert.

When we become Christians, we receive a new nature and are indwelt by the Holy Spirit; we then belong to God. However, it is important to realise that God does not reform or change the flesh, since it is irredeemable and not capable of being reformed. Instead, God gives us a new nature, so that we are now a 'new creation' [2 Corinthians 5:17]. Since the flesh had total sway over us before our conversion, it is inevitable that a fierce struggle between the flesh and the Spirit is brought on by our conversion. The most powerful expression of this struggle is given to us by Paul, in the Epistle to the Galatians:

> So I say, live by the Spirit, and you will not gratify the desires of the sinful nature. For the sinful nature desires what is contrary to the Spirit, and the Spirit what is contrary to the sinful nature. They are in conflict with each other, so that you do not do what you want.
>
> *Galatians 5:16-17*

The fierce and unremitting clash between the flesh and the Spirit leads to the internal struggle between willing and doing. As believers, we desire the things of the Spirit, and seek to please God, but the flesh is there as a very powerful influence, counteracting and resisting the Spirit. In Romans chapter seven, Paul expresses the frustration he experiences when, as a converted man, he knows he has done the things he hates in his spirit. Here we see this penetrating internal bifurcation: the conflict between the flesh and the Spirit, and the Christian as a kind of battlefield, on which the powers of the flesh and the Spirit struggle for ascendancy. But we are not the helpless and paralysed victims of the conflict between flesh and Spirit. Certainly, if we yield to the desires of the flesh, we are quickly enslaved by them. But, if we obey the promptings of the Spirit, we are then liberated, and enabled to walk by the Spirit—and thereby to subdue the flesh and to resist it.

There is a tremendous truth here, namely that, if we live by the Spirit, we shall not yield to the flesh. The way to win in the struggle with the flesh is to walk by the Spirit. If we do, then Scripture promises us we shall not indulge the desires of the flesh.

Living by the Spirit means, above all, allowing ourselves to be led by the Spirit. It involves finding the right harmony between listening and actively walking. We cannot live by the Spirit if we remain passive, just expecting the Holy Spirit to do everything. On the other hand, if we try to act without first discerning the leading of the Spirit, we are likely to find ourselves again living by the flesh and not the Spirit. Practical direction of our lives by the Spirit is often missing because we do not have the inward communion with the Lord. We do not cry out to God, longing to hear His voice. We lack frank, intimate, prolonged seeking after Him. So we end up asking God to bless what we are doing, without any conviction that we have heard from Him and are living in the Spirit, following his leading.

Living in the Spirit involves the discipline of calling to mind the truth that God is with us and that, if we abide in Christ, he will abide in us.[see John 15:4] It involves taking time to reflect on the wonderful truth of 'Christ in you'. So unremitting is the struggle between the flesh and Spirit that it is good, first thing each morning, to fix our minds on Christ.

There are so many things that are the stirrings of the flesh, which can come racing into our minds at any time of day. A girl visits her father who has left home, and spends Saturday with him. He sits before the television all day and does not ask her a single personal question. The memory of being ignored hurts. She begins to dwell on her father's lack of love to her, and to feel bitter. A wife is trying to help her husband in some task in the house but, suddenly, her husband shouts at her. She feels crushed. His shouting at her comes rushing back into her mind. A pastor is trying to explain the background to a particular project, but the only response from colleagues is a cutting remark which seems like an attack on his personal integrity. Again and again, he allows his mind to go over the scene. A son explains the details of a certain situation, but it is immediately obvious from his father's response that he has not been believed. As he recalls the conversation and his father's response, he begins to feel resentful. Experiences such as these are common enough, but they can settle in our minds and can easily be dwelt upon, so that we soon find ourselves in the midst of that fierce struggle between the flesh and the Spirit. The desire of the flesh is to indulge in the delicious feeling of having been hurt, allowing the developing resentment to assume a settled place in the heart, from which it can become a stronghold over the mind. The promptings of the Spirit, on the other hand, remind believers of how much they have been forgiven, through the blood of the cross—and that Jesus wants them to forgive, and to go on putting off the old self. For that is the only way of ensuring that the filthy garment of resentment cannot be placed around their shoulders.

In the life of the believer, an awareness of the struggle between flesh and Spirit is likely to lead to an increased understanding of past failure, and to produce a new readiness to engage in that struggle, on the Lord's side. The outcome of the struggle is going to depend on what happens in our minds; on whether we are prepared for our minds to be renewed. This is implicit in Paul's description of the old self (i.e. the old sinful nature, or flesh), which is to be cast off like a dirty garment, and the new self—which is to be 'put on', with renewal of the mind:

> You were taught, with regard to your former way of life, to put off your old self, which is being corrupted by its deceitful desires; to be made new in the attitude of your minds; and to put on the new self, created to be like God in true righteousness and holiness.
>
> *Ephesians 4:22-24*

Only if our minds are being renewed by the Holy Spirit will we be able to resist indulging the desires of the flesh.

RENEWING THE MIND

The works of the flesh are listed in the New Testament in several collections[3], and include the usual sins of the body, such as sexual immorality and drunkenness. But all lists mention various sins of the mind such as hatred, jealousy and envy. As we can see from Paul's list in Galatians, many of the manifestations of the flesh are sins of the mind:-

> The acts of the sinful nature are obvious: sexual immorality, impurity and debauchery; idolatry and witchcraft; hatred, discord, jealousy, fits of rage, selfish ambition, dissensions, factions and envy; drunkenness, orgies, and the like.
>
> *Galatians 5:19-21a*

The desires of the mind are lusts of the flesh. Jealousy,

envy, hatred, bitterness, selfish ambition and the desire to appear important can easily master us in such a way that we are being controlled by the flesh. Sadly, it is possible for a genuine Christian to enjoy the wonderful benefits of God's grace without engaging effectively in the struggle against the flesh. Recognizing our failure to grow spiritually, we may sometimes cry out: 'Oh God, change me.' But God does not change the flesh. He has given us a totally new nature. We must develop that nature by walking in the Spirit. An important key to progress in our struggle against the flesh lies in the mind. How are we thinking? Are we thinking in the old way—the way we used to think, prior to conversion, or is our mind being renewed? The reason that many battles are lost, is that our minds resist radical renewal. If our minds are neither yielded to the Holy Spirit nor undergoing the process of being renewed, then our resistance to the flesh will be only half-hearted. The flesh does much of its work by playing on our feelings and desires, and by actually discouraging clear thinking altogether. Thus we may find that we have unexpectedly lost our temper, because we failed to consider what our reaction to a potentially difficult situation should be. There did not even seem to be any temptation leading to a sinful response, but simply a natural, fleshly reaction, which meant that we simply lived for the moment. We forgot that we are a 'new creation' in Christ. When the mind is not being constantly renewed, the believer slips back into old ways, old responses—and the flesh has its way. The clearest exhortation to Christians to have their minds renewed comes in Romans:

> Do not conform any longer to the pattern of this world, but be transformed by the renewing of your mind.

> Then you will be able to test and approve what God's will is—his good, pleasing and perfect will.
>
> *Romans 12:2*

The word 'transformed' comes from the word 'metamorphosis'. We are to be changed from within, like a caterpillar undergoing the process of metamorphosis and being changed into a beautiful butterfly. The verb is in the continuous present tense in the original, indicating that we are to go on being transformed. Progression, rather than arrival, is implied and we never reach the point where we no longer need to be transformed by the renewing of our minds.

The Bible clearly teaches that, prior to conversion, our minds are fallen. We see things from our own self-centred point of view, and Satan's most powerful opposition to the gospel is to keep a grip on our minds. Paul writes:

> And even if our gospel is veiled, it is veiled to those who are perishing. The god of this age has blinded the minds of unbelievers, so that they cannot see the light of the gospel of the glory of Christ, who is the image of God.
>
> *2 Corinthians 4:3-4*

Satan blinds unbelievers through his hold on their minds. He keeps them from seeing the light of Christ and imposes his power over the world. In its most basic meaning, repentance is a change of mind, given as a gift by God to a person standing at the crossroads between heaven and hell. When we undergo the new birth through the Spirit of God, our mind undergoes a radical change about God, about

Christ and about ourselves. A veil lifts from our eyes and our minds are unclouded in key areas. We have been converted.

After conversion, our minds are not, however, totally liberated from old influences. Indeed, they now become the most fiercely contested battlefield, with all the powers of darkness striving to ensure that the old ways of thinking will not be radically changed. It is possible for a believer to receive the new life in Christ, and to have a genuine desire to please Jesus, and yet to go walking around with the 'old head'.

The process of transformation of the mind involves taking every thought and bringing it in harmony with the mind of Christ. Paul puts it like this:

> We demolish arguments and every pretension that sets itself up against the knowledge of God, and we take captive every thought to make it obedient to Christ.
>
> *2 Corinthians 10:5*

Satan has certain strongholds over our minds—strongholds which need to be captured as prisoners from the battlefield of the mind, taken captive to Christ, and then brought under his rule. A lovely illustration of this principle has been reported among certain people of Papua New Guinea, where tribal songs and dances reached such a very high pitch during annual festivals that they cried out the names of enemies from neighbouring tribes, whom they wished to kill in front of their idols. When these people were converted to Christ, they continued with their ritual, dancing and with their murder-songs, but now they shouted out, not the names of their enemies to be killed, but the names of their sins which they hated, and of which they wanted to be free. The stronghold over the mind – hatred for the enemy and planned murder – was pulled down, and these thoughts taken captive to Christ. The old way of thinking was transformed and renewed.

We need to be able to recognize parts of the battlefield of our minds which are enemy strongholds, so that we can invade them, bringing them captive to Christ. It was disturbing for me to discover that a large part of my mind remained unrenewed after conversion. I recall that for many years, as a believer, I went on believing that it was good to express my feelings and opinions without reserve, so that hypocrisy and ambiguity in personal relationships could be kept at a minimum. Speaking out what I thought, without hesitation – speaking my mind – often hurt other people. Frequently, it was little more than self-justification for my arrogance. The existence of a judgmental spirit remained hidden from me. It was an area of my mind under enemy control, and this contributed to much of my disobedience as a new Christian. Since the thoughts we think are so vital in our struggle against the flesh, as Christians we need to learn to think about ourselves in the way that God does. We need to submit our thinking to the Word of God and to the promptings of the Holy Spirit.

RECKONING OURSELVES DEAD TO SIN

Once we belong to Christ, we have the power to choose whether we will please him or whether we will grieve him. It is precisely because we are free to choose that there is such a fierce struggle. In Romans chapter six, Paul argues that a Christian is someone who has 'died to sin':

> What shall we say, then? Shall we go on sinning, so that grace may increase? By no means! We died to sin; how can we live in it any longer?
>
> *Romans 6:1-2*

As Christians, we have died to the reign, rule and dominion of sin, and are no longer under its control. We have been carried, as it were, out of the territory ruled over by Sin and transferred to the territory ruled over by Grace. The potential for this transfer came into being when Jesus died on the cross and paid the penalty for our sin. When we receive his forgiveness personally, this transfer from one domain to the other becomes an historical fact for all Christians. It has nothing to do with feelings, but with actual position and status before the living God. It may be illustrated by the example which follows.

In the 1970s, several East German citizens managed to escape over the Berlin Wall. The moment they crossed over and landed in the West they had left the regime of the German Democratic Republic (DDR) and had come under a completely different regime, that of the Federal Republic of Germany (FRG). They were either under one rule or the other; they couldn't have a foot in both camps. The wall was far too high for that! The wall between Sin and Grace is far higher than was the Berlin Wall. You are either on one side or the other.

In escaping from the Kingdom of Sin, you DIED to Sin and were no longer under its control, rule and dominion. You were freed, and then came under the rule and realm of

Grace. Christians have been taken out of the old territory (Sin), so how can they live in it any longer? It is not possible. To 'live in' means to dwell in that territory, to be under that rule, and to continue under it. But how is it, then, that we do sin, since we are no longer under the control of sin? Why do we yield to temptation? Let us return to our East German escapees. They have crossed over the wall and are no longer under the old regime (DDR). But their feelings, reactions and minds may be slow to catch up with the new historic reality of this freedom. They know, for example, that under the old regime every word spoken might be reported to the authorities and get loved ones into trouble. Consequently, they have developed a suspicious mind. They have now been brought over into a new regime but that suspicious mind comes with them. It is difficult for them to be free experientially, because the old attitudes have shaped them, making them what they are. They may, for example, imagine that letters are still censored and their behaviour watched and reported. Their thinking will be changed only gradually, and it will take time to enter into the reality of the new freedom.

For the East German escapees, it is as if an official from the old regime in East Berlin shouts across the wall and they listen and are influenced to go on behaving in the old way. Why do they do so? They do not have to. They have died to that regime. They are no longer under its control. But they listen to that voice because of habit, old influences, fear. They listen because they have forgotten that they are free from the old ruler. There are strongholds over their thinking.

In the struggle between the flesh and the Spirit, the flesh will have less success if I can remember in my mind who I have become; if I can remember that I have become a loved child of the Father, and that I have died to my old master, and now belong to my new master—Jesus Christ. Frequently, my failures in this struggle involve the failure to remember who I am and what I was before. My memory lets me down. It is crucial that Christians should realize that they have died to sin, and that its rule over them is finished for ever. They are truly free to follow Christ. Every manifestation of the flesh is an expression of their freedom to grieve the Lord Jesus, their new master.

The struggle between the flesh and Spirit is a war-like struggle and, as believers, we need to see the flesh as a hated enemy for which we can find not a single positive thing to say. God calls us to hate the works of the flesh. The flesh is to be put off, to be relentlessly fought against, to be crushed and defeated, without showing it any consideration at all. We need to remember the Scriptural perspective on the flesh—that it 'counts for nothing' [John 6:63]; that 'nothing good' lives in it, [Romans 7:18]; that it is 'hostile to God' [Romans 8:7], and that we should hate, 'even the clothing stained by corrupted flesh'[Jude 23]. Moreover, we are reminded by Paul that the appropriate way of dealing with the flesh is crucifixion:

> Those who belong to Christ Jesus have crucified the sinful nature with its passions and desires.
>
> *Galatians 5:24*

The very use of the image of crucifixion reminds us of the cross and of the words of Jesus:

> If anyone would come after me, he must deny himself and take up his cross and follow me.
>
> *Mark 8:34*

As John Stott has pointed out, our rejection of the flesh must be 'pitiless', 'painful', and 'decisive', since the very notion of crucifixion would imply not just an ordinary death but an extraordinary execution.[4]

If we are to win the war against the flesh, we must learn to hate the flesh as the active agency and seat of sin, and to hate the works of the flesh. Do we hate the fleshly desire that rises up in the heart for praise, recognition and glory? Do we hate the stirrings of jealousy and envy that seek to control our thinking? Do we hate those impure thoughts that try to persuade us into sexual sin? Do we hate the onset of resentment and bitterness, or the sudden outburst of anger from our lips? Do we hate that unexpected yielding to fear and prejudice? Do we hate that tendency of the flesh to hold on to good things for ourselves, whilst giving to God only our scarcely wanted extras and excess? Do we hate the tendency to sacrifice to God the injured and blind animals, as in the day of Malachi? [Malachi 1:7-8] Do we hate our wilful and wayward flesh, which offers to God our jumble, while we keep hold of all we value? Do we hate the principle of the flesh so much that we hate the arguments used to justify self-indulgence? Do we hate the flesh so much that, when a root of bitterness tries to establish itself in our hearts, we will cast it out? Do we remember to hate this fleshly, bitter thought?

We need to hate the flesh, because God hates the flesh. The flesh knows it is very strong. But God opposes it. He will destroy it totally at the end of time, when we step into our new resurrection bodies. Until then, we need to maintain our hatred of the flesh and give it no opportunity for reasserting its authority in our lives. As we hate the flesh, so we need to praise God for freeing us from its domination, and we need to live by the Spirit instead.

All believers need to be aware of the fierce and unremitting struggle between flesh and Spirit. But we also need to be reminded both of the amazing love of God for us, and of the power of the cross to bring cleansing and new beginnings. We should all be prepared to resist the desires of the flesh, by having our minds continually transformed and renewed by the Holy Spirit; keeping in the forefront of the memory that we have died to sin; learning to hate the flesh. The flesh must be 'put off' in such a way as to ensure that it has little opportunity for establishing its influence. In this way, old habits will give way to the new, inner life of the Spirit—with all the peace and joy of a relationship with the Lord that is not marred by habitual failure.

NOTES TO CHAPTER 1

[1] The word 'flesh' (sarx) is used by Paul to express a number of different meanings including the following: the physical body of either men or animals (1 Corinthians 15:39); the body as opposed to the spirit; life on earth (Galatians 2:20 and Philippians 1:22,24); human ancestry, without disparagement (Romans 9:5,8). Most frequently Paul uses this word to refer to the human nature as a source and expression of sinful desires (Romans 7:25; 8:4-9,12,13; Galatians 5:16,17,19). In this book the word will be used with its latter meaning.

[2] See 1 Thessalonians 5:23. The distinction between soul (psuche) and spirit (pneuma) is maintained by the writer to Hebrews. See Hebrews 4:12.

[3] See Galatians 5:19-21; Colossians 4:5-9; Romans 1: 28-29; 2 Timothy 3:2-5; Ephesians 5:3-5.

[4] See John Stott, The Message of Galatians, IVP, Leicester, pp.150-152

Chapter Two

The Struggle in the Old Testament

THE AMALEKITES AND THE FLESH

Most of the major themes of the New Testament are anticipated in the Old Testament. The struggle between the flesh and the Spirit is no exception. We can profitably treat a number of Old Testament accounts in a typological way to illuminate this, and a fascinating example is the struggle between the Israelites—the people chosen by God who are intended to reflect the life of the Spirit—and the Amalekites, who represent the flesh.

As we examine the struggle between Israelites and Amalekites, we shall become aware of many deep-seated aspects of the flesh, and also of the way in which victories over the flesh can be achieved. The Amalekites were a confederation of desert tribes located south and south-west of Judah, including the area of the Negev and the desolate regions around Kadesh, extending as far south as the wastes of Sinai. Their origins may be linked with that of the Edomites, since Amalek, the first Amalekite, was one of the grandsons of Esau.[1]

This descent is no coincidence, for there is in the Old

Testament no clearer representative of the flesh than Esau, whose early life is described in Genesis 25:19-34. Here we discover that, even while in his mother's womb, there was a struggle with his twin brother Jacob, a struggle which anticipates the struggle between the flesh and the Spirit. Esau is a man of the world, strong and rugged, a man's man who is passionate, impulsive and ready to satisfy his physical desires with little consideration for anything which does not at once appeal to his senses. Esau, the firstborn son, sold and lost his birthright, thereby revealing his indifference to the spiritual privileges associated with it. In Esau's world view, future gifts and promises cannot be enjoyed now, and so are unreal. Esau's earthiness, and his disregard for God and spiritual values, mark him as a representative of the flesh—profane and godless.

Neither is Jacob's character immediately attractive. Superficially, Jacob was anything but lovable. He was cold, calculating and a 'mummy's boy'. But, in Jacob, there was a desire for future blessing; there was a spiritual dimension. He was touched by God who, by showing him favour, caused Jacob to desire spiritual blessings. That God will bless him is suggested by the change of name from 'Jacob', meaning trickster or supplanter, to 'Israel' meaning, 'he who strives with God'.

In the last book of the Old Testament, we are reminded that God loved Jacob and hated Esau [Malachi 1:2-3]. God's hatred of Esau symbolises His hatred of the flesh. Esau, the older brother, represents the unredeemed, the one who remains in the flesh, knowing nothing other than that which comes from the sinful human nature.

God's love for Jacob, and His hatred for Esau, are worked out in the history of their descendants. The Israelites, descended from Jacob, first encountered the Amalekites, descended from Esau, in the wilderness of Sinai. Without provocation, the Amalekites attacked the weary stragglers who had become separated from the main body of Israel. The Israelites had escaped from their slavery in Egypt. They had been rejoicing in the song of Moses and Miriam over their great deliverance. They had watched their powerful enemy, the army of Egypt, perish in the Red Sea. But then the Amalekites came up from behind, to attack the Israelites at their weakest point. They remained an ongoing source of distress to the Israelites as they preyed on the stragglers, the lame, the sick, the weary and weak:

> Remember what the Amalekites did to you along the way when you came out of Egypt. When you were weary and worn out, they met you on your journey and cut off all who were lagging behind; they had no fear of God. When the LORD your God gives you rest from all the enemies around you in the land he is giving you to possess as an inheritance, you shall blot out the memory of Amalek from under heaven. Do not forget!
>
> *Deuteronomy 25:17-19*

The flesh is just like the Amalekites. Once we believers feel secure and have won some spiritual battle, we relax and recover from the exhaustion of the struggle. Then comes an attack at the point of our weakness, when we are off-guard. We are especially vulnerable to attack when we become separated from the main body of the Christian family. The attacks by the Amalekites against the weak, injured and needy stragglers show them to have been an ongoing source of distress for the Israelites. Likewise, the flesh is a constant irritant, the greatest enemy in the believer's life.

The Amalekites were the first to attack Israel and to oppose God's purposes for His people. So far, the Israelites had had to do no fighting. They had neither resisted the Egyptians whilst enslaved, nor did they have to face the Egyptian army in combat at the Red Sea. God had delivered them from slavery, bringing them through the Red Sea without a struggle on their part. In their new condition, with their new status as free men, they were now attacked. The struggle and fighting began in earnest. Until a person has been converted to Christ, there is no real struggle. The old flesh is in complete control. But afterwards the struggle commences. Now the Amalekites were 'the first among the nations'[Numbers 24:20]. They were the first in the sense that they were the most warlike (Amalek means 'warlike') and they were the first to attack Israel. The war-like nature of the flesh and its aggression can easily be forgotten. We need to remember that it is the flesh which takes the initiative in the struggle against the Spirit. It was the Amalekites who attacked Israel, not vice-versa. Peter writes in his first letter that the flesh wars against the soul [1 Peter 2:11]. The unconverted man knows nothing of such fierce fighting. Prior to his new birth he lies there, dead in his sins.

The Amalekites attacked Israel, because Israel had broken out of slavery. God was implacably opposed to the Amalekites, just as He is implacably opposed to the flesh. The final destiny of the flesh is clear from Scripture. It will be burned up by Almighty God, who is a consuming fire. Until that time, God's people are to remember how evil it is, and to fight against it. In Numbers 24:20 we read that,'Amalek was first among the nations, but he will come to ruin at last.' In Exodus 17:15, we read:'The Lord will be at war against the Amalekites from generation to generation.'

The severity of God's judgement is striking. God knows that the Amalekites are irredeemable and that their future judgement is certain.

SAUL, THE AMALEKITES AND THE FLESH

The command of God to destroy the Amalekites totally was given to Saul, Israel's first king. It was Saul's first commission. Similarly, it is the first commission to every Christian to fight the battle against the flesh and to be holy. The commission came to Saul through the prophet Samuel:

> Samuel said to Saul, "I am the one the LORD sent to anoint you king over his people Israel; so listen now to the message from the LORD. This is what the LORD Almighty says: 'I will punish the Amalekites for what they did to Israel when they waylaid them as they came up from Egypt. Now go, attack the Amalekites and totally destroy everything that belongs to them. Do not spare them; put to death men and women, children and infants, cattle and sheep, camels and donkeys.'"
>
> *1 Samuel 15:1-3*

Saul missed the opportunity of demonstrating his allegiance to the Lord by failing to obey this explicit command. He was not wholehearted in his struggle against the Amalekites. Not only did he allow Agag, the king of the Amalekites, to live[2], he also spared the best of the captured livestock, destroying only that which was weak and worthless. [1 Samuel 15: 4-9] Saul's defence to Samuel—that he simply wanted to keep the best animals and bring God the best possible sacrifices—is highly improbable.[3] The real explanation was selfishness, wanting what the eyes had feasted on even though God had said 'No'. The eyes had said 'Yes'. But even if Saul's explanation had been genuine, had he intended to keep back these animals in order to offer them as sacrifices to God, it would still have meant wanting to give God the best of what God hates the most—the flesh.

If we apply this principle—that God does not want anything from us that is fleshly, however good it seems—there are tremendous implications for our lives, both individually as Christians, and corporately, as the church. For example, we may be gifted in public speaking, and so be drawn into using that gift for God in some way. But, in so far as this gift is a natural talent unsubmitted to God, we may be depending on that skill or gift in our own fleshly strength. In so doing, we may be missing the blessing of God on the work He has called us to do. How easily church leaders can be tempted to organise the church on the basis of such natural talents and skills. We come to God holding out *our* strengths, expecting God to bless us. How greatly we need to submit to him all these things we regard as our natural talents and skills. How easily we can be tempted in this area of our strengths and talents. We need to be stripped of all that is fleshly, and come to Him acknowledging our weakness, our total dependence on Him, and our need for His strength. How different the church would be if those who were exercising public ministries were men and women who knew their total dependence on God, crying out to Him for His blessing, crying out to Him to work through their weakness.

In reality, Saul was bluffing his way through the confrontation with Samuel. He seized on the idea of sacrifice as an ad hoc explanation for the presence of livestock. It may not have been Saul's initiative to hold on to the best of the livestock. But, in yielding to the popular pressure of his army, he reveals an unpardonable lack of reverence towards the express command of God. Shifting his responsibility for disobeying God (by sparing the banned goods), from himself to the army, Saul is abdicating true leadership. He is implying that, as king, he has no real authority. Saul's tendency to give way before pressure, a weakness already evident in 1 Samuel 14, marks him as a man who is walking in the flesh, not in the Spirit.

Samuel reveals to Saul the seriousness of his disobedience, which was not forgiven and was likened to the offence of witchcraft:

> "Does the LORD delight in burnt offerings and sacrifices as much as in obeying the voice of the LORD? To obey is better than sacrifice, and to heed is better than the fat of rams. For rebellion is like the sin of divination, and arrogance like the evil of idolatry. Because you have rejected the word of the LORD, he has rejected you as king." Then Saul said to Samuel, "I have sinned. I violated the LORD's command and your instructions. I was afraid of the people and so I gave in to them...."
>
> *1 Samuel 15:22b-24*

Saul acknowledged guilt, but his attempt to evade blame indicates a lack of true repentance. He tries to justify himself. What a warning to us that we are not truly repenting if, in the same breath, we try to justify our behaviour.[4]

The very terms in which Saul justifies himself reveal the stirrings of his heart. There is no genuine repentance here, but just the fear of man—the fear of being rejected. Saul is moved by sorrow at the consequence to himself of his sin. His fear is not that he has gone against God's Word and been disloyal to the one who made him king, but that he might lose the kingdom.

King Saul is, perhaps, the most tragic figure of the Old Testament. He lost what could never be regained—the anointing of the Lord. Never again did he know that anointing. The flesh had won the battle against the Spirit. Saul lost everything, for a few cattle. Is it not true that so many Christians who start out with great zeal, and the willingness to abandon themselves to the Lord, ready to 'lose their lives' for the kingdom of God, are then distracted by the fleshly desire for status, comforts and material security? How easily we fall into the trap of placing our Christianity into a compartment and keeping it imprisoned there, living without spiritual power or real conviction.

Surely, there is intended irony in the way Saul's death is reported. It is an Amalekite who reports Saul's death to David:

> "I happened to be on Mount Gilboa," the young man said, "and there was Saul, leaning on his spear, with the chariots and riders almost upon him. When he turned around and saw me, he called out to me, and I

> said, 'What can I do?' "He asked me, 'Who are you?'" 'An Amalekite,' I answered. "Then he said to me, 'Stand over me and kill me! I am in the throes of death, but I'm still alive.' "So I stood over him and killed him, because I knew that after he had fallen he could not survive. And I took the crown that was on his head and the band on his arm and have brought them here to my lord."
>
> *2 Samuel 1:6-10*

The Amalekite's version of events conflicts with the account in 1 Samuel 31:3-6, which reports Saul as taking his own life. It is likely that the Amalekite invented his own role, anticipating a reward from Saul's successor, David. At any rate, the Amalekite did seize Saul's crown. There is a poignancy here which touches us deeply as we daily face the struggle with the flesh. Saul had begun with such great promise and such hopes for his people. He had been mightily used by God. Yet he lost the most precious possession—his crown. It was his old nature, the flesh, which proved to be his greatest enemy and his undoing. Is it not also true for us believers: that, although Satan is a cunning deceiver and powerful enemy, and the world too presses in upon us with all that our eyes can take in, the greatest enemy is within? My greatest enemy is my flesh. No one hurts me as much as I, in my flesh, hurt myself. The devil cannot take away my crown; the world cannot take away my crown—but I, in my flesh, can lose the battle; I can grieve the Holy Spirit. God's anointing can be removed.

It is David, Saul's successor as king, who cries out to God: 'Do not... take your Holy Spirit from me'[Psalm 51:11]. He is aware that the worst thing that can happen to a believer is to lose the anointing of the Holy Spirit. The Lord Jesus himself warns us: 'I am coming soon. Hold on to what you have, so that no one will take your crown' [Revelation 3:11].

How we need to cry out to God that our crown be not taken away, and that we put to death the deeds of the flesh. How we need to be on our guard and to be reminded that the flesh is the aggressor. It frequently attacks at our weakest points, aiming all the time to seize the believer's crown. The flesh itself cannot be totally destroyed in this life, but the deeds of the flesh can be put to death.[5]

Just as the flesh cannot be totally destroyed, so the Amalekites were never totally destroyed. David defeated them in battle, but there were survivors. In the days of Hezekiah (B.C. 726-693) they were slain by the descendants of Simeon.[6] But that was not their end. Some five hundred years after Saul's battle against the Amalekites and his capture of Agag, king of the Amalekites (who was put to death by Samuel), there is a reference in the Book of Esther to a descendant of Agag—Haman, son of Hammedatha the Agagite. How significant that Haman is so clearly the enemy of God's people, the Jews.[7] He wanted to kill one Jew first (Mordecai), but then to exterminate all God's chosen people. The Amalekites have always been the enemy of God's people. The flesh has always been the enemy of the Spirit.

Herod the Great, king of the Jews and yet a non-Jew, was an Idumean by descent, or an Edomite, or an Amalekite. He, too, was an enemy of God's people, who ranged himself against the true king of Israel. He was prepared to exterminate the infants in Bethlehem, in order to try and eliminate the real King of the Jews.

The battle between the flesh and the Spirit never ends

as long as we live. We have to fight that battle every day that we live for Jesus. But there is a day coming when the last battle will be fought against the flesh. All traces of the Amalekites will be wiped out from the very record of history. This is already prefigured in the complete absence of any archaeological evidence that a people named the Amalekites ever existed. In all archaeological diggings, no artefact has ever been discovered to suggest the existence of Amalekites. The only record of their existence is in the Bible. God kept His Word:

> Then the LORD said to Moses, "Write this on a scroll as something to be remembered and make sure that Joshua hears it, because I will completely blot out the memory of Amalek from under heaven."
>
> *Exodus 17:14*

Just as God has erased the memory of the Amalekites, there is a day coming in eternity when all memory of the flesh will be gone.

FIGHTING THE BATTLE AGAINST THE AMALEKITES

By examining the Israelites' struggle against the Amalekites, we can learn some important principles, which we need to apply in our own struggle against the flesh. The first of these is that without God's help this struggle is bound to fail. We can see this clearly from the results of Israel's attack on the Amalekites recorded in Numbers:

> "...for the Amalekites and Canaanites will face you there. Because you have turned away from the LORD, he will not be with you and you will fall by the sword." Nevertheless, in their presumption they went up toward the high hill country, though neither Moses nor the ark of the LORD's covenant moved from the camp. Then the Amalekites and Canaanites who lived in that hill country came down and attacked them and beat them down all the way to Hormah.
>
> *Numbers 14:43-45*

Here we see the Israelites routed because they engaged in the struggle without any word from the Lord. Indeed, Moses warned them that in this planned attack on the Amalekites the Lord would not be with them. Nevertheless, they go ahead heedless—and are defeated. This is like struggling against the flesh in the flesh, and of course can never result in victory. The only victory we Christians can ever win against our flesh is a Spirit-led victory. Frequently, we can be led astray by a recent victory in our battle against the flesh. We become proud of 'our' victory and feel assured that we have discovered the answer. Then, in that self-assurance, we fall again, discovering thereby that without the Holy Spirit there is no victory. Self-dependence always leads to defeat in the struggle. Our very strength, and our former victories, can lead us astray—into forgetting our absolute need for God's help.

The key to victory, then, is God-dependence rather than self-dependence. The key is to know deep within that I am hopelessly lost without the Spirit's direction and help. This is perfectly illustrated in Exodus:

> Moses said to Joshua, "Choose some of our men and go out to fight the Amalekites. Tomorrow I will stand on top of the hill with the staff of God in my hands." So Joshua fought the Amalekites as Moses had ordered, and Moses, Aaron and Hur went to the top of the hill. As long as Moses held up his hands, the Israelites were winning, but whenever he lowered his hands, the Amalekites were winning. When Moses' hands grew tired, they took a stone and put it under him and he sat on it. Aaron and Hur held his hands up—one on one side, one on the other—so that his hands remained steady till sunset. So Joshua overcame the Amalekite army with the sword.
>
> *Exodus 17:9-11*

It is the Amalekites, keen to gain access to the new source of water from the rock in Rephidim, who initiate the struggle against the Israelites, so as to dispossess them. It is the flesh which initiates the struggle against the Spirit. Israel did not attack the Amalekites, but the Amalekites would not leave Israel alone. As the new nature wants to experience more and more of God, and to live in peace and be still before Him, so the old nature takes up arms to suppress and defeat it.

In the struggle at Rephidim, the defeat of the Amalekites was only achieved through the uplifted hands of Moses—hands raised for the purpose of intercession.[8] While Joshua fought with the sword in the valley, Moses pleaded with God in intercessory prayer. Whilst Moses continued in intercession, his hands raised to God, the Israelites prevailed. As soon as he lowered his hands and stopped interceding, leaving Israel to fight in her own strength, the

Amalekites prevailed. How true this is for all Christians—the moment they neglect prayer they lose their dependency on God, and then the flesh prevails.

There were two aspects to the source of Israel's victory—warfare in the valley and intercession on the hilltop. Every Christian who wants to experience victory in his struggle against the flesh must be prepared both to go and fight in the valley, and to intercede on the hilltop. The battle fought against the Amalekites, in the valley, was won with the sword. The sword points us to the Bible: 'Take the helmet of salvation and the sword of the Spirit, which is the word of God'[Ephesians 6:17].

> For the word of God is living and active. Sharper than any double-edged sword, it penetrates even to dividing soul and spirit, joints and marrow; it judges the thoughts and attitudes of the heart.
>
> *Hebrews 4:12*

What an effective weapon is the Sword of the Spirit, God's Word. It is living and effective in assessing the condition of the human heart. It can throw light on the innermost nature of the believer, bringing to light hidden motives. We can deceive ourselves, covering up what we are really like, but the Bible can cut through all the deceptive layers, so that we come face to face with ourselves.

We are able to use the Word of God most effectively when we have stored it in our heart. As the Psalmist puts it: "I have hidden your word in my heart that I might not sin against you" [Psalm 119:11].

If we are going to be able to use the Sword of the Spirit effectively at times when we are attacked, we need to hide

God's Word in our hearts, ready for use. It is remarkable that in the three temptations faced by Jesus in the desert, he battled, armed with the Sword of the Spirit, replying to the tempter each time, 'It is written....' Jesus had hidden God's Word in his heart and was able to engage effectively in the battle in the valley.

To engage effectively in the valley, with the Sword of the Spirit, means recognizing weaknesses and points of vulnerability, and coming to know God's Word over those areas. If, for example, I am attacked—as nearly all new Christians are—in the area of assurance of salvation, then preparation for the battle in the valley would include learning scriptures which give assurance, and then using them at the time of attack. Similarly, if I am easily fearful and find it very difficult to share my faith, or am easily filled with worries and anxieties which tend to dominate my life as a Christian, then I need to recognise that the fear of man is a work of the flesh; that entertaining such fears is giving in to the flesh, not walking in the Spirit. I need to hide in my heart those scriptures that command me not to fear.[9]

The problem we often face is that, when we are in the valley and under attack, initiated by the flesh, we do not have that sword at our fingertips, so are ill-prepared for combat. Although the battle had to be fought in the valley with the sword, it was not won there. The outcome was decided elsewhere—through prayer. We have to appropriate victory, just as Joshua had to appropriate the Promised Land, even though victory came from God and not man.

The idea 'let go and let God' can easily deceive us into believing that we can sit back and then God will do everything. He won't! He gives the victory, but only to those who will go out and get what He gives. What Moses did on the hilltop is the key that is often left unturned in the Christian's struggle against the flesh. Moses interposed himself between God and the Israelites, praying for the needs of his people, seeking God's help and deliverance. It is significant that Moses' arms became tired. We easily become weary in intercession. In the garden of Gethsemane, Jesus had left his disciples for a short while. Returning to them, he found them asleep,

> "...Could you men not keep watch with me for one hour?" he asked Peter. "Watch and pray so that you will not fall into temptation. The spirit is willing, but the body is weak."
>
> *Matthew 26:40b-41*

The weakness of the body, and our tendency to grow weary so easily, keep us from the place of prayer. Jesus warns: 'disciples... should always pray and not give up'[Luke 18:1]. Moses grew weary in intercession, but was supported by Aaron, the high priest of Israel, and by Hur. They held up his arms until sunset, enabling Moses to persevere, ensuring the defeat of the Amalekites.

It makes a great difference in my life as a Christian if I know that while I am fighting down in the valley with the sword, there is a brother or sister standing on the hilltop and interceding for me, identifying with me in my struggle against the flesh. Be willing to become an intercessor for at least one brother or sister. The Amalekites were routed by Israel because of the work of intercession. How exciting when we, through our intercession, contribute to such victories in the battle against the flesh in the lives of our fellow believers!

All Christians have the Lord Jesus Christ, our great High Priest, who intercedes for us in heaven, and who helps intercessors in their prayers. We also have the Holy Spirit within, helping us in our weakness and in our prayer life. In the Epistle to the Romans, we read that the Holy Spirit groans for us:

> In the same way, the Spirit helps us in our weakness. We do not know what we ought to pray for, but the Spirit himself intercedes for us with groans that words cannot express. And he who searches our hearts knows the mind of the Spirit, because the Spirit intercedes for the saints in accordance with God's will.
>
> *Romans 8:26-27*

When we do not know what to pray for, the Holy Spirit intercedes for us. In the tension between the suffering of the present and anticipation of the future glory, the Holy Spirit lovingly helps us, in sighs too deep for words. In the midst of the battle between the flesh and the Spirit, the Holy Spirit brings the deepest needs of our hearts to God. We know that God will meet these needs, because the mind of the Spirit and the mind of the Father are in exact harmony.

NOTES TO CHAPTER 2

[1] See Genesis 36:12,16 and 1 Chronicles 1:36.

[2] Pride was probably behind Saul's decision to spare Agag. He probably would have been able to display the captured king as a royal slave.

[3] This feeble excuse also reveals Saul's total failure to understand that the offer of a sacrifice to God involves some cost. The contrast with David is striking, for David insists on paying for a threshing floor to be used as an altar to the Lord, even though he is offered it at no cost. He says, in reply to the free offer: ...'No, I insist on paying you for it. I will not sacrifice to the Lord my God burnt offerings that cost me nothing' [2 Samuel 24:24].

[4] Again, the contrast with David is striking. David had committed adultery and murder but he repented and made no excuses. He simply said: 'I have sinned against the Lord' [2 Samuel 12:13b].

[5] See Romans 8:12-13

[6] See 1 Chronicles 4:39-43

[7] See Esther 3:10-14

[8] See Psalm 28:2 and 1 Timothy 2:8.

[9] Scriptures such as Galatians 1:10, Psalm 118:6, Isaiah 43:1.

Chapter Three

Jealousy or Compassion

THE FIRST BEAD: JEALOUSY

Jealousy expresses the desire to have the success, popularity, possessions or worship that have come to someone else; and being thereby disturbed. God is jealous in a positive sense. If His people stray away from Him and begin to worship idols, He is jealous for their worship. In similar vein, a husband shows appropriate jealousy if his wife is flirting with another man. Jealousy, on the other hand, is a fleshly state of mind when it tends to destroy human relationships and when one is consumed by longing for that which has come to another. It may be accompanied by a sense of injustice—a grievance that the desired object has been unfairly diverted, or is about to be diverted, from the rightful possessor.

The first bead on my necklace was jealousy. I remember feeling intensely annoyed when a colleague was given a job which I would have loved to do myself. Causes for jealousy that have arisen were: when my child's success was less than that of another child; when a friend seemed to like another friend better than me; when another was praised in an area in which I have had some success. Jealousy can creep in when a brother or sister seems to sail through life, while I struggle at every stage. That jealousy is normally a fleshly state of mind is clearly revealed by Paul:

> You are still worldly. For since there is jealousy and quarrelling among you, are you not worldly? Are you not acting like mere men?
>
> *1 Corinthians 3:3*

The mark of walking in the flesh was, for Paul, jealousy and strife. The evidence that the Christians in Corinth were following their flesh and not the Spirit was that they were yielding to jealousy. Paul was disappointed that these believers, who had received the Spirit, were nevertheless living in the old way. There was the danger that their fleshly, jealous state of mind would give rise to the kind of disputes which could lead to the emergence of sects.

There is no limit to the evils that have followed close on the heels of jealousy. In the lists in which the word 'jealousy' appears in the New Testament it does so in company with words like 'murder', 'adultery' and 'envy'[Galatians 5:20 and 2 Corinthians 12:20]. It was through jealousy that Cain had been driven to kill his brother Abel. He was consumed with the thought that God favoured his brother, so he killed him. It was jealousy of the popularity of Jesus which drove religious leaders to hand him over to Pilate, and Pilate realized this only too well. Similarly, it was their jealousy of the popularity gained by the apostles which moved the high priest and his colleagues to have them arrested and imprisoned.

Many Christians have real problems struggling with jealousy. One reason is that it is something very rarely admitted. In the course of attending hundreds of prayer meetings over the last twenty years, including meetings where there has been open confession of sin, never once have I heard anyone confessing to feelings of jealousy. No one likes to admit to being jealous. People confess to not praying enough or failing to read the Bible; they confess to anger, and fear about sharing their faith; they confess to sins of the tongue and to sins of lacking love. But few appear to be aware of a need to repent of jealousy. I doubt that this means that there is little jealousy in our churches to-day.

Jealousy is perhaps the least admitted manifestation of the flesh in the life of the church today, and yet it is such a common emotion. There is the minister who feels jealous when the guest speaker is thanked and appreciated for his preaching; or when the church down the road attracts all the young people of the area; or when the church gets on well without him. There is the jealousy of those who can see someone else really growing as a Christian and hearing from God while they feel left behind; there is the jealousy of the musician who has not been invited to join the worship band; there is jealousy of the woman whom God has anointed to read the Word of God with real authority. There is jealousy directed against those who are moving in the gifts of the Holy Spirit. Indeed, in every activity in the church there are opportunities for jealousies to develop.

There are some clear biblical examples of the impact of jealousy on behaviour, including two historical episodes in the Old Testament and one of the parables of Jesus in the New Testament. In each of these episodes of jealous behaviour there are accompanying examples of compassion and kindness, as if to highlight the contrast between jealousy and compassion, encouraging those of us who struggle against jealousy to pursue its spiritual opposite of compassion and kindness.

THE BROTHERS OF JOSEPH

The Bible gives considerable space to the story of Joseph and his brothers.[1] It is clear that Joseph grew up together with his half-brothers, in an atmosphere of intense jealousy. The relationship between Rachel, Joseph's mother, and his father's other three wives was one of constant bitterness, resentment and jealousy. Such a negative atmosphere was bound to have a major impact on the sons' lives. Joseph, favourite son of the favourite wife, grew up knowing what it was to be hated by his own brothers. They, no doubt, felt the pain of being less valued and loved than Joseph who, as a teenager, had no hesitation in walking about in his distinctive coat, which set him apart from his brothers, marking him as their father's favourite son.

Joseph's desire was to be admired, but he had to cope with being hated. Indeed, so much did his brothers hate Joseph that they felt unable to speak kindly to him:

> When his brothers saw that their father loved him more than any of them, they hated him and could not speak a kind word to him.
>
> *Genesis 37:4*

When Joseph shared with his brothers the content of his God-given dreams, they were filled with even greater jealousy. Was this Joseph God's favourite as well as their father's favourite? Not if they had anything to do with it! It was insensitive of Joseph to share these dreams, but perhaps being rejected and lonely caused him to try to justify his position as the favourite son. Perhaps he yielded to the desire to make his brothers more jealous. There can be a certain fleshly delight in causing others to feel jealous of us, thereby gaining a heightened sense of importance. How careful we need to be to avoid encouraging sinful tendencies in others. Certainly, by sharing his dreams, Joseph intensified the jealousy and hatred felt by his brothers.

The brothers were so consumed by feelings of jealousy that, when the opportunity came, they decided to kill Joseph and to prove his dream false. A dead man would never be able to rule over them! But, at Judah's suggestion, rather than kill him for nothing, they decided to sell him to Midianite merchants on their way to Egypt, so making some profit out of the affair. Sin is never single in its effects, and the sin of jealousy had numerous consequences. The brothers' jealousy led them into hatred, planned murder, the sale of Joseph into slavery, deception of their father in order to hide their sin, and their father's pain of inconsolable grief at Joseph's assumed death. The effect on them of their hidden sin over many years was that they were plagued by an unrelieved troubled conscience, causing them anxiety every time something went wrong. It is so for us. Hidden jealousy towards a brother or sister in Christ gives us a troubled conscience and robs us of the peace we ought to have. Resolution cannot come until that which is hidden is brought out into the open and dealt with. God Himself sometimes arranges circumstances in such a way that our true motives are revealed. As Moses put it: '...you may be sure that your sin will find you out.' [Numbers 32:23]

This is what happened to the brothers, as they were

brought before Joseph when seeking to buy grain in Egypt in the wake of famine conditions. They were found out. After enduring great trials, testings and suffering, Joseph had been elevated by Pharaoh to the highest office in the land. He had come through the previous twenty years in a remarkable way. During his descent, from having been his father's favourite, to becoming a slave and then a prisoner, he had refused to give in to bitterness or self-pity. During this time he was being prepared by God for his coming high office. But what of the brothers? They, too, had changed during the intervening twenty years. This was revealed through the test which they are set by Joseph. Benjamin, now Jacob's favourite and Joseph's blood brother, is framed as a thief. But, instead of abandoning him to his fate in Egypt, these brothers rally around him in support, showing they are no longer consumed by hatred of the father's favourite son. Indeed, Benjamin is now the loved younger brother and they are moved by compassion and kindness towards him, not jealousy. Judah, especially, reveals the change of heart he has undergone. Twenty years earlier he had proposed profiting by getting rid of Joseph. Now he pleads to be allowed to take Benjamin's place:

> "Now then, please let your servant remain here as my lord's slave in place of the boy, and let the boy return with his brothers. How can I go back to my father if the boy is not with me? No! Do not let me see the misery that would come upon my father."
>
> *Genesis 44:33-34*

What a transformation! Here is a picture of a man who is ready to lay down his life for his brother, a man who is concerned about causing grief to his father; here is a picture of compassion and kindness which contrasts strikingly with the earlier jealousy and hatred that had led to Joseph's enslavement to Midianite traders.

Through testing initiated by Joseph, the brothers were shown to be not the same men as twenty years earlier. Furthermore, they were set free from the guilt of the past, through the generous love and forgiveness of Joseph. The account of Joseph's brothers shows us that those who have been consumed by jealousy and hatred, through acknowledgement of previous guilt [2], can be transformed into people who are compassionate, kind and free from jealousy. It is impossible to feel both compassion and resentment towards the same person simultaneously.

The emotions exhibited in the story of Joseph are certainly not unknown in our days. Parents who favour one of their children above the others can do immense harm to those children, who come to feel unloved, unvalued, unwanted—in some ways not as worthy as the favourite. This can apply even where such favouritism is not open, and is perhaps even hidden from the parents themselves. Often, those who felt unloved as children carry that sense of worthlessness into their adult lives, together with open or repressed jealous feelings towards the favoured sibling. They can also develop a tendency easily to become jealous of any attention or love being shown to others in their circle, and to look over their shoulders to see whether they are being properly appreciated.

In the biblical account of Joseph, jealousy and all its attendant evils eventually came out into the open. Then they could be dealt with in a way that brought forgiveness, wholeness and reconciliation, where previously there had been lack of peace and prolonged guilt. We need to learn from this striking episode that our jealousies must come out into the open and be dealt with, if we are to lead godly lives.

SAUL, DAVID AND JONATHAN

A remarkable biblical example of jealousy is that of King Saul in his relationship with David. There could hardly be a more striking contrast to that jealousy than the compassion and kindness which Jonathan, Saul's son, shows toward David.

Saul is rejected as king over Israel, both because of his disobedience regarding the Amalekites and because of his unrepentant heart-attitude. He tried to play with God's grace, wanting to look right in the eyes of Samuel, and with God, in front of the people. There is no inner repentance, no change of heart, no cry from the heart for restored fellowship with God, no longing that the Spirit of God would stay upon him. The result of this failure to repent was the departure of the Holy Spirit from Saul and the arrival of an evil spirit:

> Now the Spirit of the LORD had departed from Saul, and an evil spirit from the LORD tormented him.
>
> *1 Samuel 16:14*

It is clear that Saul is not only suffering from depression as a result of the departure of the Holy Spirit—he is now afflicted by an evil spirit, which has its own personality. The evil spirit comes from outside, and is given access to his inner being.

It is foolish to try and explain away the reality of this spiritual being which afflicted Saul. If as believers we refuse to die to self but, rather, indulge the flesh, we open up ourselves to possible affliction by demonic powers. It is remarkable, but not without precedent, that God Himself sends the evil spirit to Saul. God also sent a lying spirit to Ahab's prophets:

> Micaiah continued,"Therefore hear the word of the Lord: I saw the LORD sitting on his throne with all the host of heaven standing around him on his right and on his left. And the Lord said, 'Who will entice Ahab into attacking Ramoth Gilead and going to his death there?' One suggested this, and another that. Finally, a spirit came forward, stood before the LORD and said,'I will entice him.'
> 'By what means?' the Lord asked.
> 'I will go out and be a lying spirit in the mouths of all his prophets,' he said.
> 'You will succeed in enticing him', said the Lord. 'Go and do it."
>
> *1 Kings 22:19-22*

If we turn away from God as our power and life-source, we are inviting evil powers to come and fill the void. They are thereby able to gain access into, and influence over, our lives. Saul, plagued by the evil spirit, provides a picture of a man who has known something of the power of God, has tasted of the Holy Spirit, but has pulled away from Him and is out of communion with Him. When Paul warns the Christians in Ephesus that their struggle is not against flesh and blood—but against the powers of darkness—he implies that these powers of darkness seek to gain access, an access that can be denied by refusing to live the self-life; walking in the Spirit rather than in the flesh. Only through the name of Jesus Christ can the powers of darkness be cast out once they have gained access. This deliverance is possible because Jesus totally defeated and humiliated them on the cross.

It is not difficult to see that jealousy is the appropriate name for the spirit which afflicted Saul. He was in bondage to this spirit of jealousy from the moment God allowed the spirit to enter him. To a remarkable extent, Saul's whole life was controlled by stirrings of jealousy from this time on.

The situation which first gave rise to Saul's intense jealousy was David's victory over Goliath, or rather the popular song which celebrated that victory, elevating David above Saul:

> When the men were returning home after David had killed the Philistine, the women came out from all the towns of Israel to meet King Saul with singing and dancing, with joyful songs and with tambourines and lutes. As they danced, they sang:
>
> 'Saul has slain his thousands, and David his tens of thousands.'
>
> Saul was very angry; this refrain galled him.
>
> 'They have credited David with tens of thousands,' he thought, 'but me with only thousands. What more can he get but the kingdom?' And from that time on Saul kept a jealous eye on David.
>
> *1 Samuel 18:6-9*

The worm of jealousy, directed by the evil spirit in Saul,

now begins to consume this man and to destroy him. His jealousy was deeply aroused by the popular song because he knew that he himself should have stood up to Goliath. He was the tallest Israelite and had the best armour. David had gone out unarmed, but with the Spirit of God upon him. Saul's consciousness of his fear before Goliath heightened his jealous feelings towards David, who was clearly God's man, and who had the Spirit of the Lord—just as once Saul himself had known the Spirit upon him. The women's song carried the implication that David rather than Saul was God's man. Had not the prophet Samuel told him that God had already chosen a successor to Saul, and that this choice was irrevocable?

> '...He who is the Glory of Israel does not lie or change his mind; for he is not a man, that he should change his mind.'
>
> *1 Samuel 15:29*

Saul had been Israel's national hero and had been acclaimed as a great warrior. As he listened to the words of the popular song, he felt he had been supplanted by a man who had proven his courage and was chosen by God. From the day Saul heard that song, the evil spirit of jealousy allowed him little peace, drawing him into hatred and outbursts of uncontrollable anger, as well as creating in him an overriding fear that he would lose his kingdom to David.

> The next day an evil spirit from God came forcefully upon Saul. He was prophesying in his house, while David was playing the harp, as he usually did. Saul had a spear in his hand and he hurled it, saying to

himself, "I'll pin David to the wall." But David eluded him twice. Saul was afraid of David, because the Lord was with David but had left Saul.

1 Samuel 18:10-12

Saul was driven to attempted murder, almost managing to spear David to the wall. One sin in the life of a man always attracts other bed-fellows, and what begins as jealousy can easily grow into hatred, rage, fear and even murder.

Since Saul recognized that God's hand was with David in all David did, his own drastic opposition to David was really his opposition to God. This is the blindness to which the spirit of jealousy led Saul. He imagined that he could upset God's plans by killing David. A dead man could not take the kingdom away from him, so Saul would kill David and then nothing would come of God's plan. But killing David proved impossible, precisely because God was with David. How blinded Saul must have been to oppose God's chosen one! Every failure to eliminate David simply confirmed to Saul that he was fighting against God, and intensified his own fear of ultimate failure. Yet Saul, in spite of all the evidence of God's special protection for David, continued to try to destroy him. How easily we are blinded by our sins so that we cannot see the utter futility of fighting against God Himself.

How utterly self-destructive it is to make oneself the enemy of God's man, the enemy of the one of whom it is said: 'God is with him'. The sin of jealousy, and related sins, blind us to the truth that we are destroying ourselves. The only course available for those who have been driven by jealousy is to come to self-awareness and repentance before being consumed by this sin, and, if the jealousy has been of a chosen servant of God, to understand that this amounts to opposing God Himself.

The spiritual opposite of jealousy is compassion and kindness. Nowhere in the Old Testament does one see more moving expressions of human kindness and compassion than in Jonathan, Saul's son. Saul had initially loved David when David first entered the king's service, ministering to him in music. But his love turned into jealousy and hatred. Jonathan, by contrast, never wavered in his love for David. He was happy to see his friend honoured in the popular song, and was grateful that Israel had been saved through David. He must have been conscious of his own failure to stand up to Goliath's challenge. But he did not feel threatened by David's success. He admired and loved David. This is the more remarkable since Jonathan knew very well that David would assume the throne which belonged to Jonathan by right of inheritance. So kind was Jonathan that he protected David against his father's murderous plans, at the cost of alienating his own father.

There is an unselfish quality to Jonathan's love for David which is the mark of genuine friendship, and which is strong enough to ward off any potential stirring of jealousy in Jonathan's mind. Whilst Saul was consumed with jealousy and hatred, his son maintained a deep loyalty to David throughout and allowed himself no jealous imaginings. Once we give way to jealousy, then compassion and kindness are quickly driven out. Soon there is room only for jealousy and associated works of the flesh. Jonathan's last meeting with David, while Saul is pursuing David in order to attempt to kill him, reveals his uncompromising stand in maintaining his compassion, kindness and love toward David—and his consistent rejection of the temptation to be jealous of the one who would take his throne:

> While David was at Horesh in the Desert of Ziph, he learned that Saul had come out to take his life. And Saul's son Jonathan went to David at Horesh and helped him find strength in God. "Don't be afraid," he said. "My father Saul will not lay a hand on you. You will be king over Israel, and I will be second to you. Even my father Saul knows this."
>
> *1 Samuel 23:15-17*

The selfless compassion of Jonathan for David is an example of the positive qualities of the man of the Spirit, while the jealousy and uncontrolled passions of Saul exemplify the negative qualities of the man of the flesh.

THE PRODIGAL AND THE OLDER BROTHER

The most penetrating study of jealousy in the New Testament is to be found in the picture Jesus draws of the older brother, in the parable of the prodigal son. Jesus tells this parable in order to show the Pharisees and religious leaders of the day that their critical attitude to him—for welcoming and eating with sinners—was, at the deepest level, a critical attitude to God, who welcomes the homecoming of repentant sinners. That this is the underlying purpose of the parable is clear from the context.[3]

The older brother's attitude toward the father's welcome for the returned prodigal gives us insight into the inner stirrings of jealousy. Why should his father be so glad over the return of his brother, who had squandered everything and was now returning home in disgrace with nowhere else to go? The older brother cannot understand his father's compassion and joy at such a homecoming. Surely, the appropriate and just response would have been to reprimand this son for bringing disgrace and shame on the family? It is the father's love and compassion for the prodigal which arouses the jealousy of the older brother. His jealousy and anger are aroused as he compares his own faithful service ('I have been slaving for you all these years') with his brother's profligacy and irresponsibility. As he indulges his mind in this comparison he is consumed with a sense of his father's injustice. To lavish such love, mercy and compassion on the prodigal—and even to hold a great feast for his homecoming, when he himself had never received such a reward, though he was the one who deserved to be rewarded—was to give way to feelings of jealousy. Because the older brother's heart was full of jealousy, there was no room for compassion for his brother's situation, but rather a giving way to envy, pride, bitterness, hatred and self-deception. Here, we are shown clearly that it is impossible to feel both sympathy or compassion and jealousy simultaneously. Eating away at the older brother's heart is a seething resentment against his father, that he should so overlook all his faithful service and focus his loving attention on one who was totally undeserving, one whom he would not even acknowledge as his own brother, but refers to angrily as 'this son of yours.'[Luke 15:30]

The picture of the older brother is a disturbing one. It is the picture of a man who has become spiritually cold, unfeeling, hard and self-righteous; a man who tries to do what is right— not out of love, but because of duty. It is the picture of a man who is living in the father's house without seeing what a great joy it is to be near the father; it is the picture of a man who has forgotten that he is a son rather than a servant. Here is a man who feels he has been slighted because his own brother has entered into the joy of being a son, loved and forgiven, while he seems unable to enter into the joy and liberation of sonship. He prefers to see himself as one who has *earned* the favour of his father. It is a painful picture; this is a man with a deep wound which festers away and will not heal. It is the wound of feeling unloved while seeing a brother being loved. The older brother believes he has earned and deserved his father's love, but is unable to enter into the experience of being loved—because love cannot be earned or deserved. He refuses to go in and rejoice together with his father and brother. He cannot enter into such rejoicing, for jealousy has crowded out from his heart all those things that facilitate rejoicing.

Just as the jealousy of Saul was contrasted with the love, kindness and compassion of Jonathan, so here in this parable the jealousy and anger of the older brother are contrasted with the compassion and love of the father. How stark is the contrast between the great, merciful and compassionate heart of the father and the jealous, bitter and unsympathetic spirit of his elder son.

At a spiritual level, jealousy is really an expression of hostility to God, since the jealous person focuses his attention on someone else's success and achievements, aggrieved that this other has been blessed by God. Jealousy is really an attack on the justice of God and an expression of resentment against God for blessing others. The jealous person craves for himself the blessings bestowed on the favoured one. Jealousy expresses the insecurity of feeling unloved by God. Why has God endowed that person with gifts of preaching, of music, of prophecy, of evangelism, of success, wealth, good looks or a smooth path in life? God must love that person in a special way that he does not love me, and every time I see that person I am reminded of God's love to him and the absence of God's love to me. Such are the inner workings of the poison of jealousy.

Jealous feelings towards others can very readily be rationalized by being attached to faults—real or imagined—in that 'favoured' person. It is not difficult to see that the effect of jealousy in the church (or family or workplace) is to bring dissension, conflict and restlessness. God's purpose for the church is to mould it into a loving family, where members are drawn together and learn to love one another, valuing their inter-dependence. Satan's purpose for the church is to destroy it, by drawing members apart in rivalry and antagonism. He uses jealousy to produce disorder, dissension and prevailing moods of disharmony and a spirit of criticism.

Every Christian needs to combat the tendency to jealousy, which is there as an aspect of our flesh and is a temptation for all. Jealousy is frequently tolerated as something 'natural' – not really wicked. Success in battling against the temptation to be jealous is likely to be limited, unless we realize how much God hates jealousy, and how unsparingly Satan uses it as a key tool. The believer will not make progress in the battle against jealous thoughts and behaviour until he repents of past failures in this respect. There needs to be an acknowledgement of any past yielding to jealousy, and then repentance—a turning from every known jealous thought and behaviour pattern, bringing it to the cross.

Following on from repentance, a number of steps will be helpful in the ongoing struggle against jealousy for the believer:

1. Stop doubting God's love for you. Spend time thanking the Lord that you are His treasured possession, that He chose you and died for you.

2. Stop doubting God's justice. Remember that God's ways and thoughts are perfect:'As the heavens are higher than the earth, so are my ways higher than your ways and my thoughts than your thoughts'[Isaiah 55:9]. If you have thought it unfair that other believers have been apparently more blessed than you: repent, and confirm your faith in the perfect justice of God.

3. If a jealous idea comes creeping into your mind, then take authority over that area of your mind that is under attack. Take authority over that thought in the name of Jesus Christ. It can be helpful to speak out, saying: 'I rebuke you jealousy, in the name of Jesus Christ, and recognize that you come from the evil one.' You need to take a grip firmly, casting out the jealous thought that tried to ingratiate itself into your mind and justify itself with many rationalizations. Remember to 'take captive every thought to make it obedient to Christ'[2 Cor.10:5].

4. Remember that the spiritual opposite of jealousy is compassion and kindness. If your heart is full of compassion and kindness towards a person, you will not feel jealous towards him or her. Pray for compassion and

kindness so to fill your being that you can genuinely pray for blessing on the one who has irritated you.

5. If you come to the point of being able, like Moses, to rejoice in the other person's accomplishments or blessings[4], then you will know that you are winning the battle against jealousy.

6. Pray along the following lines:

'Father God, I acknowledge the jealous thoughts in my mind as wrong and inexcusable. Please forgive me and renew my mind about X, that my heart may be filled with compassion for him.'

NOTES TO CHAPTER 3

[1] See Genesis 37-50.

[2] See Genesis 44:16. Here Judah acknowledges that their guilt has been uncovered, clearly meaning the guilt of selling Joseph into slavery twenty years earlier.

[3] See Luke 15:1-3

[4] On hearing that two men were prophesying in the camp, Joshua wanted to stop them, but Moses said, 'Are you jealous for my sake? I wish that all the Lord's people were prophets and that the Lord would put his Spirit on them.' See Numbers 11:29.

Chapter Four

Covetousness or Love

THE SECOND BEAD: COVETOUSNESS

Greed is the craving after food, material objects, or position and honour, and is evidence of the lust of wanting to have, to possess. It is most severely condemned in Scripture. Paul even demanded that believers avoid all social interaction with those believers who are greedy[1]. To greed, covetousness adds the desire for goods which are owned by someone else. It involves allowing one's eye to gaze upon and desire a forbidden object— forbidden in that it is owned by one's neighbour. The object appears especially desirable precisely because it appears to be beyond reach. Covetousness is a sin of the heart which lies at the root of many other sins, such as adultery, theft and murder. It is the most basic of all sins, for it speaks of the corruption of the heart. It does not allow anyone to say 'not guilty'. It is instructive that, in his analysis of the way in which he became aware of sin in his own life, Paul was convicted of the reality of his sinfulness by the Commandment 'You shall not covet'.[2]

Probably the single most significant thing about covetousness or greed is that it is identified in the Bible with idolatry. Paul writes:

> Put to death, therefore, whatever belongs to your earthly nature: sexual immorality, impurity, lust, evil desires and greed, which is idolatry.
>
> *Colossians 3:5*

Greed and covetousness take over our hearts, leading us away from God into idolatry. By setting our hearts so much on having things, we can abandon undivided loyalty to the true God, for those things crowd God out.

Jesus warned against the danger of covetousness as the door into idolatry.[3] The unwholesome desire — to take up the goods of life that surround us and to give way to an appetite that demands more and more— is unwholesome and evil, precisely because it so quickly assumes central place in our lives. It supplants the place which we, as believers, should give to serving God. It is not that material things are bad. Nowhere does the Bible make such an assertion. On the contrary, material goods should be enjoyed—but we should not yearn for them in such a way that their enjoyment is our goal. The covetous person does not become an idolater by valuing and enjoying earthly possessions, but by making a god of them, in the sense that he seeks not merely to derive pleasure from them, but through them to gain security, peace of mind and meaning. The covetous person who is a believer tries to do what is impossible: he tries to serve God and money.(4) Attempting to do both, he is inevitably separated from God and falls into idolatry.

The second bead of my necklace was covetousness which is, of course, closely allied to jealousy. From time to time, I have desperately wanted to own some object or other. When I was an academic it was a large and impressive library of books, and a house in a fashionable neighbourhood. As a clergyman it has been the financial security of 'money in the bank'and the recognition that comes with visible success. When I have actively sought to gain these things, my sense of closeness to the Lord has invariably been diminished.

In a barren time in my life, when nothing much seemed to be happening in my work and I felt restless and desperate at the way time was passing, God showed me the importance of being willing to accept my circumstances. Soon after I surrendered this desire to be successful, He led me to a completely new place, full of promising opportunities.

There are many examples in the Bible which bring out the true nature of covetousness as the desire to HAVE, to possess, to own that which belongs to others. We will look at two examples from the Old Testament and one from the New Testament.

AHAB AND NABOTH; DAVID AND BATHSHEBA

Ahab, king of Israel, returned to his country palace in Jezreel, having fought a successful war against the Arameans. He then spent his time improving his property and grounds. As he did so, he saw an adjoining vineyard belonging to Naboth—and the desire for it was awakened. It would make an excellent kitchen garden. The fact that this object was forbidden did not deter Ahab from seeking to get it. Like Eve, who reached out after the forbidden fruit, Ahab reached out for the forbidden land, hoping to buy it off Naboth or get it by exchange. In setting his heart on

Naboth's vineyard, and in offering to buy it for more than it was worth, Ahab was really tempting Naboth to break God's law, which did not permit an Israelite to sell any part of his inheritance.[5]

Naboth resisted the temptation to sell or exchange his family inheritance, and was courageous enough to resist the king's wishes, refusing to ignore the command of the law. He was determined to hold on to the plot of land that had been owned by his fathers for generations. Having set his heart on getting the vineyard, Ahab was devastated by this brusque denial of his offer. He retreated into his palace, frustrated, angry and full of desire for that vineyard. He retired to his bed, sulking there like a spoilt child who has been thwarted. Lying on his bed, refusing to eat, Ahab indulged his covetous thoughts. In his feeling of frustration, that vineyard became more and more desirable to him. So when his shrewd wife Jezebel arranged to have Naboth judicially murdered, thereby making the property available, Ahab went along with her plan. At the mercy of his ravenous desires, and in his weakness, Ahab yielded to the temptations of his wife. Upon Naboth's death by stoning, Ahab took hold of his vineyard, and enjoyed his possession of it. But he was interrupted. The interruption by Elijah is a kind of sign that covetousness always brings forth its own fruit. Far from being able to enjoy his new prize possession, Ahab's peace was disturbed by Elijah.

No believer has ever envied his fellows without going through a similar disturbance. It is not possible to lust after something belonging to my neighbour and, at the same time, to experience peace of mind. Covetousness is itself an expression of restlessness, rooted in dissatisfaction and discontent with what one has. The covetous thoughts are simply intensifying that restless discontent. To be dissatisfied with what God has given is to deny oneself peace of mind.

Of course, the sin of covetousness and its attendant sins can be forgiven upon repentance, but their implications may well continue long after one has been forgiven. Ahab's sin, and his abuse of arbitrary power to get the desired object, had shattering implications for his family. Although he himself was spared, because he humbled himself before God[6], the outworkings of his sin are seen in the terrible deaths suffered by his children.

It is amazing to think that Ahab, the king of Israel, who had so much of everything, should set his heart on a vineyard that belonged to another. And yet is this not similar to the case of King David who lusted after Bathsheba? David set his heart on having the wife of one of his subjects. He saw Bathsheba, and was determined in his heart to have her. The sin of coveting was the basic sin, and the adultery was the external outworking of that sin. David stretched out his hand to get Bathsheba and he abused his kingly power in order to arrange for her husband to be killed, just as Jezebel, with Ahab's consent, abused the royal power in order to get rid of Naboth [7]. In Nathan's parable, rebuking David for his adultery with Bathsheba[8], the tremendous injustice of David's actions comes out. Did he not have beautiful wives? Why lust after a woman who is the loved wife of another man? Ahab's lusting after the sole vineyard of Naboth is very similar to David's lusting after the only wife of Uriah. The tremendous force of coveting, of giving way in one's heart to a selfish whim, is at the root both of David's adultery and of Ahab's theft and his murder of Naboth.

David repented, acknowledging that he had sinned against God. He offered no excuse for his sin. His repentance was genuine, and he was totally forgiven. But his sin was not without consequences, which were with David for the rest of his life. The examples of Ahab and David confirm that covetousness is at the root of much evil, and remind us that we need to be on guard against this internal manifestation of the flesh, which can so easily spill over into external manifestations. But even if covetousness remains in the mind and heart without outward expression, it is no less evil for that. In God's eyes it is an abomination, for it is idolatry.

ACHAN

While Ahab feasted his eyes on the property belonging to another man, Achan allowed himself to covet goods which belonged to God. Following forty years of wandering in the desert, the Israelites entered the Promised Land, winning a glorious victory over the fortress of Jericho. There was every sign that the Lord brought Israel this great victory. Furthermore, there was a great general anticipation that Israel stood at the start of a new era in her history. Never had Israel been more confident of future victory.[9] But, following closely on the heels of the victory at Jericho, Israel suddenly stumbled inexplicably at Ai. This was a much smaller fortress standing at the top of a hill which Joshua needed to take, in order to gain control of the central highlands beyond Jericho and the Jordan. At the news of the defeat by the people of Ai, Joshua fell down before the Lord in despair and came close to blaming the Lord for

Israel's defeat. It is strange that Joshua failed to consider the possibility that Israel herself might be to blame through sin. After all, was it not disobedience against God which had caused the desert wanderings for forty years? Sin had come into the camp and was the reason for Israel's defeat at Ai. The Lord had allowed Israel to be defeated, because she had acted unfaithfully in one respect.

Israel had agreed to 'devote' all of the spoils of Jericho to the Lord. The spoil was 'holy' to the Lord and came under the 'ban' of total destruction. Achan saw some of the things devoted to the Lord, and desire for them was aroused in his heart. The sin began with looking and then took over his mind. He saw, he coveted and he took. Achan did not hold back his hand from taking that which belonged to God. He stole from God, then he hid what he had stolen. Here is a pattern which has repeated itself endlessly throughout history. Seeing the forbidden object, coveting the object, taking it, and then covering it over in order to hide the sin. When Achan saw the fashionable Babylonian garment, and the silver and gold, he admired them. Although he knew they belonged to God, and were therefore forbidden, he allowed his mind to become occupied by these things—so much so, that they became his heart's desire. How could it be wrong to take them? No one else would be deprived, since it was not a question of sharing out these goods. They were for God alone—and God surely would not mind such a trifle going to Achan. By hiding his stolen goods, Achan revealed that they quickly become a source of anxiety.

Nevertheless, Achan thought he could hide his sin, and that it would never be discovered. Certainly, Joshua did not know that the anger of God had been kindled against Israel because of the sin of just one Israelite. Achan thought that his sin of covetousness and theft was a private matter. But sin is never just a private matter. Thirty-six men had to die because of Achan's sin. Israel had to suffer a humiliating defeat at the hands of the Canaanites. This defeat at Ai would be a source of comfort to all Israel's enemies, and a source of anxiety to the whole camp of Israel, aware that God's hand of blessing on taking possession of the promised land had been lifted.

Because it was in God's plan to go on blessing Israel in her occupation of the land of Canaan, He exposed the sin of Achan, enabling it to be dealt with.[10] This one sin had to be dealt with before Israel could continue to advance. What a salutary lesson that is for every local congregation. Is there sin in one member—in me—that is blocking God's blessing on the church? Am I slowing or hindering the blessing of God on the church, because of concealed sin? Is there greed and coveting and envy in my heart, holding back the working of the Holy Spirit in the church? What a responsibility. Achan thought his sin was personal and private, of no concern to anyone else. But how we live as Christians inevitably has a knock-on effect. There are no sins which are entirely private and without repercussions for our Christian family.

Achan stole from God about thirty four hundred years ago, and Israel suffered. Some thousand years later, the majority in Israel were stealing from God in failing to tithe—to give one tenth of their income. This matter is taken up by the prophet Malachi, writing when the exiles had returned to Jerusalem, had rebuilt the temple and walls around Jerusalem, but had wandered from God's way. Malachi warns the people to return to the Lord, but they declare their ignorance of any wrong-doing:

"...Ever since the time of your forefathers you have turned away from my decrees and have not kept them. Return to me, and I will return to you,"says the Lord Almighty.
"But you ask, 'How are we to return?'
"Will a man rob God? Yet you rob me.
"But you ask, 'How do we rob you?'
"In tithes and offerings."

Malachi 3:7-8

Malachi reveals that the nation is stealing from God by not bringing in the tithes and offerings set out in the Law [Leviticus 27:30]. By giving the tithe, Israel could acknowledge the truth that the earth belongs to the Lord with everything in it. By failing to bring it, Israel was trying to cheat God and was consequently under a curse:

'You are under a curse—the whole nation of you—because you are robbing me.'

Malachi 3:9

Israel was repeating the sin of Achan in stealing from God, and she was suffering just as she suffered for Achan's sin. No doubt greed and covetousness tempted people to stop bringing one-tenth of their income. How gracious of God to restore Israel, after Achan's sin had been dealt with, and how gracious His promise to Malachi that Israel would be restored and abundantly blessed upon resumption of tithing.

"Bring the whole tithe into the storehouse, that there may be food in my house. Test me in this," says the

> LORD Almighty,"and see if I will not throw open the floodgates of heaven and pour out so much blessing that you will not have room enough for it. I will prevent pests from devouring your crops, and the vines in your fields will not cast their fruit," says the LORD Almighty. "Then all the nations will call you blessed, for yours will be a delightful land,"says the Lord Almighty.
>
> *Malachi 3:10-12*

ANANIAS AND SAPPHIRA

There are many interesting parallels between the story of Achan and the story of Ananias and Sapphira in Acts chapter five, not least in the time sequence of both stories. The great blessing of Israel's victory at Jericho is followed by the sin of Achan. Sin spoils that victory, God judges Achan and the way is made clear for future blessing. In the case of Ananias and Sapphira, the sequence of events is remarkably similar. There comes first the great outpouring of God's Spirit at Pentecost and a period of blessing for the church marked by daily conversions, signs and wonders, and the unity among the believers so real that it included sharing their personal possessions. But covetousness now raises its head to spoil the situation. And just as Achan's sin was against God—he stole from God—so Ananias and Sapphira's sin was against God. They lied to God. Their sin, too, was followed by the judgement of God, so that the blessing on the church might continue and not be held up. Satan's intention was to restrain the advance of the church through the deceit of Ananias and Sapphira, but God overruled

Satan's plans by revealing this sin, judging it and enabling the church to progress in power.

There is every reason to believe that Ananias and Sapphira were genuine believers, and that Satan, having failed to silence the disciples by external threats from the religious authorities, now adopts an internal approach, seeking to subvert the church from within.[11] The sin of Ananias did not lie in the amount of money he kept back from the sale of the land. It was, rather, the envy he felt towards those who were admired in the Christian community for their whole-hearted giving. Ananias and Sapphira coveted the honour in which such men as Barnabas were held, and were prepared to lie about their giving in order to be thought equally generous. They coveted spiritual prestige. Had Ananias and Sapphira sold their house and then brought one third of the proceeds, saying 'we are giving one third to the church and keeping the rest', that money would have been welcomed—but, of course, they would not have been a part of the inner circle of those who gave all they had. Their sin was really hypocrisy—pretending to be more generous than they really were. They coveted the reputation of those who were admired for giving their all. As they brought the money, they wanted to bask in the praise of men: 'Aren't they generous to give the proceeds of their house? Those two really trust God for everything!' To enjoy such praise, whilst at the same time wanting to enjoy their money, is to indulge in the worst form of hypocrisy—religious hypocrisy. The lie of Ananias and Sapphira to the church was not a lie to men, but a lie to God. Ananias and Sapphira had tried to deceive the apostles, but in doing so had tried to deceive God, so real was the apostles' awareness of the presence and power of God the

Holy Spirit in their midst.

Just as Achan's covetousness and theft were revealed by God Himself, so the deceit of Ananias is exposed by the Holy Spirit. Ananias and Sapphira sinned against the love and truth that had come about in the brotherhood of the early church.

The true nature of their sin is unmasked in the interrogation by Peter. This was not a sin into which they had fallen on the spur of the moment. Husband and wife had together agreed on the deception. The way in which both Ananias and Sapphira were struck dead served as an object lesson for the church. It was a warning that God sees the state of the heart, however much we conceal it from our brothers and sisters; and that He is resolutely against all deceit, unreality and double mindedness, as well as against covetousness and envy.

God's prompt judgement of Ananias and Sapphira, and the zeal with which God watched over the purity of the early church, is rather sobering when we consider that their sin is easily recognisable in the church today. Pretending to be what one is not in the local church; being untrue to the congregation and lacking genuineness and integrity in relationships is all too common. How easily we Christians can slip into pretending to be great givers, pastors, carers, or to be really devoted and holy. Even though we may know that on closer inspection such claims could not be sustained, yet we can easily be tempted to enjoy a positive reputation for any of these spiritual virtues. I know I can, anyway.

Ananias and Sapphira coveted a good spiritual reputation, envying those who basked in such sunlight. At the same time, they wanted to enjoy the means of the world. Such duplicity and hypocrisy are not so uncommon in the church of today, and should make us hesitate before self-righteously condemning the failure of Ananias and Sapphira.

COVETOUSNESS VERSUS LOVE

There seems to be no end to the kind of things that we set our hearts on and covet. We may covet our neighbour's money, house, car, holidays, appearance, clothing, spiritual reputation, spiritual gifts, as in the case of Simon Magus[12]; or status and power, as in the case of Absalom who coveted his father's crown and kingdom.[13] To covet is to allow one's heart to become so full of desire for an object that one falls into idolatry, which is the condition where one gives to that object the attention which only God should receive. The root of covetousness is the failure to love God, the failure to be content, and the failure to love one's neighbour.

Our devotional life is profoundly influenced by covetousness. God can hardly be expected to manifest His presence to a person who already has his being focussed on some other desired object. If a vessel is filled with water, it is unreasonable to ask for that same vessel to be simultaneously filled with wine. First it must be emptied of the water; then it can be filled with wine. When we try to come to God with covetous hearts, we need first to acknowledge our sin, repent, and be emptied of the wrong desires, so that our hearts can then be filled with a true desire for God and the things of His kingdom. If we hang on to those wrong desires for self, we shall never know what it is to have a wholehearted desire for the living God.

The positive spiritual opposite to covetousness is love—love for God and love for one's neighbour. A heart that is full of love for God, and thankfulness to Him, cannot covet. It is impossible both to envy someone and simultaneously praise God with a genuinely thankful heart. It is also impossible both to love my neighbour and simultaneously covet his possessions. This is because covetousness focusses on what the person *has*, rather than on what he *is*. If I covetously envy my neighbour for some material object or spiritual gift, then I am focussing on him not as the person he is—not on his being—but on his having. I see him in terms of what he has got, wanting this for myself. Not only do I fail to love my neighbour if that is how I see him, but I am not loving God, since I am then failing in the area of contentment. Love and covetousness are mutually exclusive. I have found it very helpful to ask the Lord to fill my heart with love for the person towards whom I am tempted to feel envy, at the very first stirrings of that impulse.

Covetousness is the inward sin of putting self at the centre, of seeking self-gratification. It is the demand that self be satisfied, stimulated by the fleshly drive of getting, and evoked by looking enviously on the things owned by others. For a Christian it involves having divided loyalties, and it can only be resisted once this is recognized. The destructive power of covetousness can be resisted effectively only by wanting God so much that there is no room in our hearts for covetousness. But what steps can we take to develop such a longing for God? One helpful step is to develop the 'grace of giving' [2 Corinthians 8:7] to the point where the lust for getting loses its appeal.

Giving is a grace, because it can release us from the principle governing the world, the principle of getting. The

Macedonian Christians in Paul's day had learnt this secret of giving and were enabled, in spite of their 'extreme poverty', to give towards a collection for the poor believers in Jerusalem, 'as much as they were able, and even beyond their ability'[2 Corinthians 8:4]. Here we see in these believers the true opposite of covetousness: hearts that are bursting to give, to love. In such hearts there is no room for covetousness. Such generous giving brings an inner release and peace, a freedom from being enslaved to the principles of the world.[14]

When the returned Jewish exiles were diverted—by the desire for home comforts—from their initial enthusiasm in giving themselves to the task of rebuilding the temple in Jerusalem, they began to face hard times, with low harvest yields: an economic recession.[15] This meant there was now, in any case, nothing left over for restoring the temple. But when, despite these conditions, the exiles repented and began to set their hearts on giving themselves to restoring the temple, they were given the greatest reward any believer can receive. As their own homes became secondary to them and God's kingdom assumed the first place in their hearts, God said: 'I am with you'[Haggai 1:13]. There is no greater encouragement in our struggle with the flesh than to hear the living God say to us: 'I am with you.'

When we learn to love God and our neighbour it means that we have learnt to give generously of ourselves—our time, energy, money—and the effect of such giving is that we are released from the prison of covetousness. Then there is a kind of bursting loose in our lives: there is a proper flow, whereas before there was only a trickle. It is like a lamp being lit in our lives when we practise this 'grace of giving', but it is a lamp that can go out if we return to clutching our possessions to ourselves, and fall back into being consumed by self-absorption.

When tempted to give way to greed and covetous imaginings, it is good to bring this at once to God and to pray for forgiveness.

Please Lord help me to turn from this selfishness and fill my heart with love for X that I may see him not as the owner of things, but with your eyes of love.

The next step is to praise God for the things He *has* given you, and the good things you *do* enjoy—and a growing sense of contentment will come.

NOTES TO CHAPTER 4

[1] See 1 Corinthians 5:10 and 1 Corinthians 6:10

[2] See Romans 7:7-9

[3] See Luke 12:15

[4] See Matthew 6:24, where Jesus warns that it is not possible to serve two masters; 'You cannot serve both God and money.'

[5] See Leviticus 25:23 and Numbers 36:7

[6] Ahab humbled himself. He 'lay in sackcloth and went around meekly' in response to Elijah's pronouncement of judgement. See 1 Kings 21:27-29. The fact that God responded by delaying the

judgement is a remarkable sign of His mercy to a man who had distinguished himself by doing more evil than any previous king of Israel.

[7] The details of this affair are recorded in 2 Samuel 11.

[8] See 2 Samuel 12:1-2

[9] See Joshua 5-7

[10] Achan and all who belonged to him were stoned to death. See Joshua 7:24-26

[11] The verb 'kept back' is identical with that used in the Greek Septuagint version of the Old Testament, to describe the action of Achan in taking hold of a portion of what was devoted to God.

[12] See Acts 8:9-20

[13] See 2 Samuel 15

[14] The giving of ourselves, our time and money, is not in order to get this inner release and peace, otherwise it would be another kind of getting. But the fear of loss to self, the fear of the consequences of self-denial, is so great in all of us that the Bible gives us strong words of encouragement to be givers. See Haggai 1:12-13; Malachi 3:10-12; Luke 6:38; 2 Corinthians 9:6.

[15] See Haggai 1:1-11

Chapter Five

Pride or Humility

THE THIRD BEAD: PRIDE

I had never seen myself as a particularly proud person but, as I struggled with the Lord over this bead of my necklace, I came to see how mistaken I had been. Even today, the Lord challenges me in this area of my life, through my failure to respond well to criticism. Pride flares up when another criticises my work, my ideas or anything important to me. 'How dare they treat me like this?' is so often my initial response. I remember being mortified by a letter criticising my ministry in one church I led. It took my breath away. I felt anger for weeks whenever I thought of it, as though I had been struck. The Lord helped me to see that my reaction was wrong and that I needed to be humbled, and to learn to respond to criticism in a more godly way.

Another area on which the Lord put His finger was pride due to natural gifts and advantages. I was proud of being from a well-educated, successful background, being fairly articulate and capable. I had to be weaned from depending on my strengths, through being put into impossible situations.

Pride is the very root of all other sins, so much so that it is impossible to commit a sin without falling into pride. It is an expression of the flesh which draws us into believing that we can manage without our maker, without God; that we need neither God nor other people; that we can manage on our own and do not need help. Pride flows from the kind of self-sufficiency which gives no room for God, and seeing dependence on and trust in Him as weaknesses rather than virtues.

> In his pride the wicked does not seek him; in all his thoughts there is no room for God. *Psalm 10:4*

The proud do not allow themselves to be moved by God, because their hearts are so full of self that there is no room for God to visit there. Pride is the attitude of heart which snatches the crown from God and puts it on self. At its deepest, it is acting from oneself, and for oneself independently of God, making a god of self and refusing to act within the limitation of one's creaturely status. This very refusal to accept such limitation involves a denial of reality, resulting in deceitfulness. In the words of Habakkuk, pride involves a failure in 'uprightness'. Referring to the king of the Babylonians, Habakkuk writes:

> See, he is puffed up; his desires are not upright—
> but the righteous will live by his faith—
> indeed, wine betrays him; he is arrogant and never at rest.
> Because he is as greedy as the grave and like death is never satisfied,
> he gathers to himself all the nations and takes captive all the peoples. *Habakkuk 2:4-5*

The key thought here is that the man who is puffed up with pride is in his basic nature 'crooked', with an inner conceit in his heart separating him from others and persuading him of his superiority over them. This tendency to overvalue oneself and undervalue others leads to a state of restlessness, and to the desire for more power and influence. There is an accompanying destructive aspect of pride leading to discontent, self-destruction and ultimately hell. That pride is devilish is clear from the very character of Satan. Pride is the essence of Satan's being. In Ezekiel, it seems that Satan, pictured as the king of Tyre, was at one time very wise and perfect in beauty, anointed by God and perhaps the highest of all the angels. But Satan became discontent with his created status. There was no longer any joy in being God's servant:

> "Your heart became proud on account of your beauty, and you corrupted your wisdom because of your splendour.
> So I threw you to the earth; I made a spectacle of you before kings."
>
> *Ezekiel 28:17*

Satan's heart was lifted up with pride in his beauty and wisdom, so he was cast from God's presence. Satan turned from creaturely submission to the creator to independent self-assertion. A description of pride is given by the prophet Isaiah [chapter fourteen], and it may well be that his words not only describe the arrogance of the king of Babylon, but also carry a veiled reference to Satan.

How you have fallen from heaven, O morning star,

son of the dawn!
You have been cast down to the earth, you who once laid low the nations!
You said in your heart, "I will ascend to heaven;
I will raise my throne above the stars of God;
I will sit enthroned on the mount of assembly,
on the utmost heights of the sacred mountain.
I will ascend above the tops of the clouds;
I will make myself like the Most High."[1]

The five-fold 'I will' reveals the depth of self-assertion and total independence from God. Not content to be God's chief officer, Satan insists on the honour of being god himself. The devilishness of sin is, according to Martin Luther, revealed by a change in the first words of the Decalogue, from 'I am the Lord your God', to 'I am my Lord and my God'. The desire to become god was at the root of Satan's fall, and it is therefore not surprising that Adam's fall, planned by Satan, was caused by a similar temptation to pride. The tempting prospect that '...you will be like God' [Genesis 3:5] aroused in Eve a surging forth of pride that has since then never been extinguished in mankind, and which expresses itself in the ongoing determination to be morally independent of God. Pride is devilish because it is Satan's very essence, and because Satan is constantly repeating his first temptation to draw mankind away from dependence on God.

It is the rebellion against God implicit in human pride that God hates. Certainly, there is no manifestation of the flesh more strongly condemned in the Bible than the sin of pride:

Whoever has haughty eyes and a proud heart, him

will I not endure.

Psalm 101:5

The Lord Almighty has a day in store for all the proud and lofty,
for all that is exalted....

Isaiah 2:12

He [The Lord] has scattered those who are proud in their inmost thoughts.

Luke 1:51

God opposes the proud but gives grace to the humble.

James 4:6

God opposes the inner heart attitude that sets itself against His very being and sovereignty. Our natural way of thinking is to condemn lawbreaking but to excuse heart-attitudes that do not necessarily find expression in visible offences. It would, for example, be quite conceivable for someone to say; 'he is a good man but rather proud', while it would be more surprising to hear someone say 'he is a good man but a thief.' Open sins are more offensive to us because they may bring disgrace upon us. But God hates and opposes pride because this is the heart attitude which sets itself most against God.

The Lord detests all the proud of heart.
Be sure of this: They will not go unpunished.

Proverbs 16:5

Pride is devilish and deadly, for it bars the way to God.

God's whole plan of salvation humbles us, for it reveals that we can be saved and made whole only by God's grace through faith in Jesus Christ; and faith involves saying, 'Help me Jesus—I need you, for I am hopelessly lost without you.' A Christian can sing from the heart:

> 'When I survey the wondrous cross
> on which the prince of glory died,
> My richest gain I count but loss
> and pour contempt on all my pride.'

Pride is deadly because it is *the* disposition which keeps people from God, resisting the cross and saying, 'I do not need Jesus, even if others may need him.' Pride opens wide the gates of hell and blocks entry into heaven. In matters of salvation, the people who reckon they qualify on their merits will discover by that very fact that they do not. To claim God's approval on the basis of one's position or achievement is a positive disqualification.

The opposite of pride and self-exultation is humility and, just as God opposes the proud, so He looks down with favour on the humble:

> Though the LORD is on high, he looks upon the lowly,
> but the proud he knows from afar.
>
> *Psalm 138:6*

> "This is the one I esteem: he who is humble and contrite in spirit,and trembles at my word."
>
> *Isaiah 66:2b*

Humility involves removing self from one's thoughts,

words and feelings to such an extent that one no longer readily places trust in oneself. Positively, it first requires me to realize that without God I am nothing, then to move into a position of complete dependence upon Him. Humility is acquiescence in one's position of creaturely dependence on God.

The struggle between the flesh and the Spirit should involve taking off the dirty garments of pride, arrogance and self-reliance, and putting on the garments of humility, and serving others in a spirit of security in the Father's love. The small child, who has no status in the world, and looks to its father for security with total trust, has the kind of dependent attitude towards God we need to develop—if we are going to deal with the secret and hidden pride that clings to all of us. There are many examples of pride in some of the characters of the Old Testament.

PHARAOH

In Exodus, Pharaoh is presented as such a proud and haughty ruler that he comes across as a type of Satan. He resolutely refuses to let the Israelites leave Egypt:

> Pharaoh said, 'Who is the LORD, that I should obey him and let Israel go? I do not know the LORD and I will not let Israel go.'
>
> *Exodus 5:2*

Pharaoh, who was himself an object of his people's worship, and totally sure of himself, had no fear of God. He made the mistake of assessing the power of Israel's God by observing the existing status of the Israelites. 'Their God must be weak, since they are my slaves,' he reasoned. His pride was expressed in wilful resistance to God. In spite of the evidence of the great power of Israel's God, through the successive plagues, Pharaoh would not give Him glory. He hardened his heart, so his heart was further hardened by God. The failure of the plagues to move Pharaoh's heart revealed the depth of his pride, self-will and defiance of God. After losing the Israelite slaves through blood redemption, Pharaoh tried to recapture them and bring them again under his control. He totally failed to be humbled by the evidence of God's power, remaining convinced that he could still prevail against Him. That is the pride of unbelief. 'I do not know the LORD and I will not let Israel go.' This is the response of many who hear the Gospel but close their ears to its command that all men should repent. Continuation in the pride of unbelief brings further hardening of the heart and, finally, condemnation. [2 Thessalonians 1:8-9]

DAVID

God hates the pride of the unbeliever, but also vigorously opposes pride in His own people. A fascinating example of a godly man falling into pride is King David. His case is all the more instructive for we are not encountering David as a raw youth, but as a mature man at the end of his life. In 2 Samuel 22, David sings a great song of praise to God as his rock, fortress, shield and deliverer. He gives glory to God for all his past, and he delights in God's kindness and gentleness to him. In 2 Samuel 24, however, we read that, in one of his last acts as king of Israel, against all advice, David insists on taking a national census. This was at a time of peace, when Israel had established secure borders and was no longer threatened by any foreign powers. Apparently, David wanted to take pride in Israel's strength. He succumbed to the temptation to place his trust in the number of young fighting men, rather than in God's hand upon Israel. This was the pride of the flesh drawing security from military power. David wanted to impress the surrounding nations with a fine show of strength. In his old age, David forgot that Israel was a nation under the protective hand of the Lord, not a nation needing to depend on superior military power.

David's sin is that of a successful man who has forgotten that his victories were based on God's grace. It is the sin of a man who wants to feel secure in the size of his armies. David's aspiration for self-sufficiency is a sure sign that he has given way to pride. All the more strange since, almost more than any other figure in the Bible, David had, throughout his life, learned to depend on God to deliver him and to win his battles.[2]

The example of David is a good reminder that we do not always behave 'in character', and that the struggle against pride is an ongoing one, which even those closest to the Lord have to go on fighting. It is a daily struggle to avoid slipping back into pride.[3] Success can make us blind to the danger of pride, even where pride has previously been dealt with in a godly way.

David's fall into pride resulted in personal suffering, which began with deep conviction of sin [4] and the realization that he had let God and others down. Instead of deriving pleasure from knowing the precise military strength of Israel, David is disturbed by a heavy sense of guilt. For us, as for David, conviction of sin is God's work, signifying that God has not abandoned us but wants us to be restored to full fellowship. This process involves our taking sides with God against ourselves. It means humbling ourselves:

> "...If my people, who are called by my name, will humble themselves and pray and seek my face and turn from their wicked ways, then will I hear from heaven and will forgive their sin and will heal their land."
>
> *2 Chronicles 7:14*

The way out of pride is always by humbling ourselves before God, acknowledging our sin and turning from it. Then the Lord pardons us and blots out our sin, restoring fellowship with Himself, even though some of the consequences of our pride may still have to be worked through. As in the case of David, we may have to see others suffering the consequences of our pride, which reminds us that sin matters, even though we can be forgiven and our guilt removed.

David fell into pride after being greatly used by God to establish righteous rule, political stability and secure borders for Israel. Success in any venture brings with it the temptation to become proud. The dangers are brilliantly spelled out for us in the Book of Deuteronomy, and we will be wise to hide these words in our hearts:

> When you have eaten and are satisfied, praise the

> LORD your God for the good land he has given you. Be careful that you do not forget the LORD your God, failing to observe his commands, his laws and his decrees that I am giving you this day. Otherwise, when you eat and are satisfied, when you build fine houses and settle down, and when your herds and flocks grow large and your silver and gold increase and all you have is multiplied, then your heart will become proud and you will forget the LORD your God, who brought you out of Egypt, out of the land of slavery. He led you through the vast and dreadful desert, that thirsty and waterless land, with its venomous snakes and scorpions. He brought you water out of hard rock. He gave you manna to eat in the desert, something your fathers had never known, to humble and to test you so that in the end it might go well with you. You may say to yourself, "My power and the strength of my hands have produced this wealth for me." But remember the LORD your God, for it is he who gives you the ability to produce wealth, and so confirms his covenant, which he swore to your forefathers, as it is today.
>
> *Deuteronomy 8:10-18*

This warning is so apposite, because the flesh invariably forgets God's role in bringing material blessings and security to believers. The Israelites forgot that the very land of Canaan was a gift from God, recalling instead how hard and well they had fought for this land, and how they deserved their prosperity after the years of wandering in the desert and after their military campaigns against the enemy. It is when we are blessed with prosperity and success that we are most inclined to say presumptuously: 'I and my skill and hand accomplished this.'

The pattern of falling into pride as a result of experiencing success applies in the spiritual realm just as much as in the material realm, and is no less abominable in God's sight. It is, for example, easy to become proud of one's successes in evangelism if one is working in an area where there has been much hard prior sowing and preparation for reaping. Soon the evangelist becomes convinced that his methods, his approach and his gifts are the crucial ingredients rather than the work of the Holy Spirit, even though he may continue to believe in and proclaim the sovereignty of God in evangelism.

A sign that one has fallen into spiritual pride is that one begins to see oneself no longer as part of the body of Christ, but as somehow detached from it or above it. Believers who have fallen into spiritual pride look at their own church fellowship as if they were looking at it from outside, notwithstanding that they are members of that fellowship. Feelings of superiority creep in. A further development may be that they may find it difficult to submit to those in authority in their church. Somehow its rules and regulations do not apply to them in the same way as to others. A whole church may fall into pride because of its size or reputation. Sometimes the Lord removes the blessing to bring us to our knees before Him.

HEZEKIAH

Hezekiah was one of the few good kings of Judah, clearing idolatry out of the temple and out of the land.[5] After being told that he was dying, he was miraculously healed by the Lord with an accompanying sign to point to his certain healing. The king of Babylon sent envoys, ostensibly to congratulate Hezekiah on his healing, but really to make a practical assessment of how useful Judah would be as an ally against Assyria. Hezekiah, flattered that he should be so well-known in far-off Babylon, told the envoys the story of his miraculous healing and showed them the full extent of his possessions, wanting to impress them and wanting them to report well of him. Hezekiah, by showing them all the wealth of the nation, was in effect saying that Judah had resources and could give very valuable aid in any campaign against Assyria.

Just as David had been deceived into trusting in his military strength for security, so now Hezekiah placed his trust in a possible future treaty with Babylon. This eagerness for such a treaty incurred God's wrath:

> In those days Hezekiah became ill and was at the point of death. He prayed to the LORD, who answered him and gave him a miraculous sign. But Hezekiah's heart was proud and he did not respond to the kindness shown him; therefore the LORD's wrath was on him and on Judah and Jerusalem.
>
> *2 Chronicles 32:24-25*

After his miraculous healing, Hezekiah promised to walk humbly with God, but became so elated and excited by his recovery that he slipped back into pride, putting his trust in treaties with foreign powers, rather than in the Lord who had healed him.

Times of spiritual blessing are just the times when we

are most tempted to become proud, imagining that the blessings are related to our gifts or efforts rather than to God's grace. Just as Hezekiah fell into the trap of boasting about his healing, then about the possessions of the nation, so we can slip into spiritual boasting about spiritual blessings or accomplishments and this can entice us into feelings of self-importance. Before we know it, we have abandoned our position of dependence on the Lord.

UZZIAH

King Uzziah was, like Hezekiah, one of the few good kings of Judah. After being on the throne for some forty years, he suddenly fell into the sin of pride:

> But after Uzziah became powerful, his pride led to his downfall. He was unfaithful to the LORD his God, and entered the temple of the LORD to burn incense on the altar of incense. Azariah the priest with eighty other courageous priests of the LORD followed him in. They confronted him and said, "It is not right for you, Uzziah, to burn incense to the LORD. That is for the priests, the descendants of Aaron, who have been consecrated to burn incense. Leave the sanctuary, for you have been unfaithful; and you will not be honored by the LORD God." Uzziah, who had a censer in his hand ready to burn incense, became angry. While he was raging at the priests in their presence before the incense altar in the LORD's temple, leprosy broke out on his forehead.
>
> *2 Chronicles 26:16-21*

After Uzziah had become powerful, he fell into pride. Here we see again the dangers which accompany success. This was no sin of impetuous youth, but rather the sin of a man approaching sixty, a man of power and authority. How could he fall into such a sin of presumption? The example of Uzziah serves as a warning to the mature, to leaders and to those exercising spiritual ministries. They should never think of themselves as anything but ordinary people graciously empowered by the Lord. We never reach such a level of spiritual maturity that we are free from danger of succumbing to the temptation of pride.

Uzziah's sin was to take on the role of priest as well as king, thereby trying to concentrate all power and influence in his own hands, ignoring the divinely ordered conditions for the priesthood. His punishment—leprosy—was for the sin of pride, for a heart lifted up against God and hungry for more power.

The temptations for the successful to swell up with pride are just as acute today as in the days of King Uzziah. Not only are we tempted to become forgetful of God's grace to us, imagining that our abilities or efforts have been decisive in taking us so far, but we may well seek to increase our influence or authority in the church or community. How difficult it is to stop feeding this pride, and how difficult to stop trying to stand out and be noticed; to stop drawing attention to ourselves. How difficult we find it to rejoice when others around us are praised and valued highly while we are overlooked; how hard we find it to avoid slipping back into pride when we ourselves are praised:

> The crucible for silver and the furnace for gold, but man is tested by the praise he receives. *Proverbs 27:21*

THE PURSUIT OF SELF-GLORY: MIRIAM

Self-glory is closely related to pride, but is sought by those who lack self-confidence and are insecure, as well as by those who are proud and feel superior to others. An interesting example of the pursuit of glory for self is found in Miriam.

The book of Numbers describes the attitude of Miriam and Aaron towards their brother Moses, after God had enabled seventy elders to prophesy. Miriam was a prophetess and had taken a leading part in the song of deliverance, sung to celebrate the crossing of the Red Sea. It was in her prophetic gift that Miriam sought glory for herself, but she did so in a hidden way by grumbling against Moses, her brother, that he seemed to act as if he were the only one through whom God spoke. Who is Moses, to make such exclusive claims? Had he not married a Cushite wife—hardly a great recommendation for a prophet of the Most High God?

> Miriam and Aaron began to talk against Moses because of his Cushite wife, for he had married a Cushite. "Has the Lord spoken only through Moses?"they asked. "Hasn't he also spoken through us?" And the Lord heard this.
>
> *Numbers 12:1-2*

Miriam seems to have been the leader of this grumbling against Moses, and Aaron went along with his sister's complaint, just as he had gone along with the people's demand for a golden calf. Miriam wanted more glory for herself as a leader, and for Aaron.[6] She wanted, together with Aaron, to be on equal terms with Moses. She simply used the ethnic background of Moses' wife as an excuse to gossip, to get at Moses, and to challenge the notion of his spiritual pre-eminence.

We can recognise, in Miriam's heart, desires which are not uncommon, especially the desire to be recognised as outstanding, to be seen as the one through whom God speaks and works. Miriam is driven by the fleshly craving for greater recognition.

In her desire for glory to accrue to herself, Miriam is ready to undermine the authority of Moses. It was ironic that Moses, more than any other man in the world, was concerned not for his own glory but for God's glory. He was 'a very humble man, more humble than anyone else on the face of the earth'[Numbers 12:3]. More than anyone, Moses depended totally on God.

There are many Miriams in the church today—not only in the area of music and prophecy. The desire for self-glory, for prominence and acclaim, is easily mixed with an intense jealousy against those thought to have too prominent a role. The resulting resentment in those who feel undervalued and marginalised is an enormous hindrance to true worship and fellowship.

Miriam's striving for self-glory, and her challenge to the exclusive authority of Moses, was punished with leprosy which meant she was temporarily shut out of the fellowship of the camp. She was, therefore, publicly shamed and could only be received back after her healing. The terrible punishment would have helped Miriam to see how great her sin was against Moses and God. Do we recognise that our striving after glory for self is a great sin which can easily hold back our church? Do we recognise God's loving hand of discipline upon us when He humbles us? If only God would show us some of His glory so that we might be humbled.

SEEKING GOD'S GLORY: DANIEL

In no character of the Old Testament is there a more faithful rejection of self-glory, and a constant aspiration for glory to come to the one and only true God, than in Daniel. Here is a man with much opportunity to take glory to himself. On one occasion, Nebuchadnezzar, the king of Babylon, had a troubling dream. He invited his astrologers and wise men to tell him his dream and interpret it. Of course no-one could do such a thing. After God had revealed the contents of the king's dream and its interpretation to Daniel, Daniel praised God, then revealed the dream to Nebuchadnezzar. But to ensure that no honour or glory came to himself, but that God alone should be given glory, Daniel explained to the king:

> "...No wise man, enchanter, magician or diviner can explain to the king the mystery he has asked about, but there is a God in heaven who reveals mysteries. He has shown King Nebuchadnezzar what will happen in days to come. Your dream and the visions that passed through your mind as you lay on your bed are these...."
>
> *Daniel 2:27-28*

Daniel continued to insist he was nothing more than God's instrument for revealing the dream, and had no special wisdom of his own:

> "As for me, this mystery has been revealed to me, not because I have greater wisdom than other living men, but so that you, O king, may know the interpretation and that you may understand what went through your mind."
>
> *Daniel 2:30*

Although the pagan king did bestow honour on Daniel, it was certainly not sought by him. In any case, the king had learnt that it was Daniel's God who deserved all honour and glory:

> The king said to Daniel, "Surely your God is the God of gods and the Lord of kings and a revealer of mysteries, for you were able to reveal this mystery."
>
> *Daniel 2:47*

In the person of Daniel we get a glimpse into the heart of a man who is truly godly, a man who has lost all fear of men and all desire to receive the praise and honour of men, but is taken up with the glory of God and longs for God to be given all glory. Daniel was delighted that God was glorified in the midst of a pagan nation.

Daniel, who was greatly beloved of God, had an inner spiritual life which focussed so much on God that he was not preoccupied with his own role in serving God. His eyes were not on himself—how *he* could serve God—but on the majesty, the glory and awesomeness of God. The greatness of God's power and majesty, His holiness and splendour, got through to Daniel in such a way that he never forgot the greatness of his God in everyday life. Daniel's inner spiritual life was such that he had one inflexible goal that could not be shaken—to seek to bring glory to God. He had come to a point of true humility, with an awareness that without God he would be nothing. Only if we develop our own inner spiritual life as Daniel did, can we resist the fleshly tendency to self-glory.

PRIDE AND HUMILITY IN THE NEW TESTAMENT

Since pride is at the root of all sin, it is not surprising that humility, its opposite, is a vital and frequently recurring subject in the New Testament. One of the most powerful contrasts drawn by Jesus between pride and humility occurs in his parable of the Pharisee and the Tax Collector. [Luke18:9-14]

The Pharisee of the parable clearly lives a better moral life than the tax-collector, and he knows it. He is respectable, law-abiding and religious. He can thank God for doing positive things in his life. He finds within himself things that make him feel proud, as he considers his past record. Yet his prayer never gets off the ground. It is not accepted, precisely because he thinks he can stand before God. Whilst recognizing that he does have some faults, he compares himself favourably with the tax-collector, clearly feeling good about himself as a result. It is this complacency, and the attitude of superiority to others, which displeases God. A proud look at our brothers and sisters in church makes us think we are better than they are, and that our faults are small by comparison. The tax-collector does not compare himself with anyone else, not even with colleagues who are, perhaps, more dishonest. He does not look down on anyone else, but looks up to God, his conscience burdened. As he stands before God, he sees the filth of his life, and any comparisons with others do not enter his mind. He singles himself out as THE sinner, and is alone with God. In God's presence he begins to know himself. The decisive thing, when we stand in the presence of God, is not so much our past record as our present attitude to God.

Sometimes when we spend time in prayer, it seems as though we hardly get through to God. Is this not often because we come with the disposition of the Pharisee rather than the Tax-collector, and we lack the self-knowledge that the Tax-collector had in looking solely to God, seeing his deep need for repentance, forgiveness and dependence on Him? We need to come to the end of ourselves, as the Tax-collector did. But our pride intervenes, showing us something about ourselves that is not so bad. Then we come like the Pharisee, complacent, and ready neither to abandon our self-reliance, nor to become truly dependent on God.

In Christian circles, people are very often evaluated according to their gifts, abilities, leadership potential and hard work. But God thinks most of the man who thinks least of himself, because it is through such a man that God can bring glory to His own name.

Jesus' own teaching on humility is remarkable. He opens his Sermon on the Mount with the words: 'Blessed are the poor in spirit'[Matthew 5:3]. This is the foundational beatitude for without it there can be no blessing. All the other virtues arise out of our right attitude to ourselves and to God—out of humility. Our spiritual failings will, on close examination, turn out to be at the same time a failing in humility. To be poor in spirit is to be conscious that we are unable to achieve anything of lasting value by ourselves, and to become empty of self, so that we cease to place any reliance upon any natural advantages we may have—whether of birth, nationality, natural temperament, education, position in life, material resources, etc. All these things can so easily control us when we look to them. But those who are poor in spirit have laid aside all such old grounds of confidence. They have become aware of their emptiness through looking to God. Their desire is that they might be filled with the Holy Spirit and be used as vessels by God. They want to live in true dependence on Him, as a small child lives dependently on its parents.

The apostle Paul learnt the secret of resisting pride. He had tremendous powers of intellect, and other great natural advantages, which gave him good reasons for being confident in the flesh. But, when he arrived in Corinth, he felt very inadequate for his task there:

> "When I came to you, brothers, I did not come with eloquence or superior wisdom as I proclaimed to you the testimony about God. For I resolved to know nothing while I was with you except Jesus Christ and him crucified. I came to you in weakness and fear, and with much trembling. My message and my preaching were not with wise and persuasive words, but with a demonstration of the Spirit's power, so that your faith might not rest on men's wisdom, but on God's power."
>
> *1 Corinthians 2:1-5*

He had learned the secret of becoming poor in spirit, so God could use him powerfully as an emptied vessel, with glory going to God rather than to Paul.

The most outstanding example of humility is the life of

the Lord Jesus Christ. Jesus was willing to lay aside the glory of his divine majesty, to become man and to serve mankind. While he lived on earth, men refused to recognize him as God, but reviled, despised and crucified him. The humiliation and self impoverishment of the Son of God is seen in the incarnation and passion of Jesus, and in the way he adopted the place of total dependence on God the Father. Jesus' self-renunciation was with a view to the welfare of others. He was ready to enter a strikingly humble manner of existence, taking the form of a servant and allowing himself to be abused and humiliated, rather than ruling in power and great majesty. He became weak and defenceless— 'the Lamb of God who takes away the sin of the world'[John 1:29]. In Jesus we have the supreme example of humility, the only example in human history of a man who knew no pride in his heart:

> Your attitude should be the same as that of Christ Jesus: Who, being in very nature God, did not consider equality with God something to be grasped, but made himself nothing, taking the very nature of a servant, being made in human likeness. And being found in appearance as a man, he humbled himself and became obedient to death—even death on a cross!
>
> *Philippians 2:5-8*

The humility of Jesus is seen not only in his incarnation and passion, but right through his earthly life, in which may be discovered an astonishing level of acknowledged dependence on the Father. Humility is the heart-attitude which consents to let God be all. This is just what Jesus did, and especially in the Gospel of John we find Jesus making it absolutely clear, time and again, that he always acted in dependence upon the Father. Andrew Murray points out in his book *Humility*, how unceasingly he [Jesus] uses the words *not* and *nothing*, of himself.[7]

'I tell you the truth, the Son can do nothing by himself.' *John 5:19*

'By myself I can do nothing....' *John 5:30*

'I do not accept praise from men' *John 5:41*

'For I have come down from heaven not to do my will but to do the will of him who sent me.' *John 6:38*

'My teaching is not my own. It comes from him who sent me.' *John 7:16*

'I do nothing on my own but speak just what the Father has taught me.' *John 8:28*

'I have not come on my own; but he sent me.' *John 8:42*

'I am not seeking glory for myself....' *John 8:50*

'The words I say to you are not just my own....' *John 14:10*

'These words you hear are not my own; they belong to the Father who sent me.' *John14:24*

Here, in the totally dependent attitude of Jesus to the

Father, we can see perfect humility. What a striking contrast with the self-exaltation of Satan, who sinned against the sovereignty of God. Jesus submitted himself totally to the Father, and the Father worked through Jesus as He has never before worked through any other.

One of the most powerful examples of Jesus' willingness to serve is the footwashing scene, described in John chapter thirteen. The disciples were on their way to Jerusalem and had been arguing about human greatness. As they arrived for the Last Supper in the upper room, they found a jug, basin and towel,but no slave to wash all the dirty feet. No-one moved, so Jesus got up and took the towel and, kneeling before each disciple, washed their feet. Here, Jesus taught the disciples that the condition for advancing in God's kingdom is the opposite of that of the world. To efface oneself and put on the 'apron of humility' is the condition for greatness in God's kingdom. Here, the way up is down.

Peter's initial protest against the washing of his feet sounds very humble, but is in fact a manifestation of hidden pride:

> He [Jesus] came to Simon Peter, who said to him,"Lord, are you going to wash my feet?" Jesus replied,"You do not realise now what I am doing, but later you will understand." "No," said Peter, "you shall never wash my feet." Jesus answered,"Unless I wash you, you have no part with me." "Then, Lord," Simon Peter replied,"not just my feet but my hands and my head as well!" Jesus answered,"A person who has had a bath needs only to wash his feet; his whole body is clean. And you are clean, though not every one of you."
>
> *John 13:6-10*

We may well imagine that Peter's train of thought was: you wash my feet— never! I am not like the others here, Jesus. I am too sensitive for you to wash my feet. The others may not mind, but I do. Pride is the poison that ruins Peter's service, and Jesus lets him know that he must deal with it. Peter agrees and is washed.

Why was Jesus so ready to pick up the towel, while none of the disciples moved? He was not concerned about his reputation with men, whilst the disciples were worried about their image: how they would be seen by the others. They were more concerned with their reputation than with their character. There is a beauty, purity and amazing humility in the love of Jesus that is simply breathtaking— the Son of God washing the dirt from his disciples' feet whilst they are all too status conscious to do the job! Jesus had nothing to prove to man, but was perfectly secure in the Father's love. This made his service totally free from any hidden motives.

THE STRUGGLE AGAINST PRIDE

Whilst we may conquer some sins, pride will always remain a danger as long as we live. We must be constantly vigilant in our struggles to resist it. Pride even feeds on our very virtues and spiritual progress. Unless we actively fight against pride, it will steal in, and self will be lifted up. If we are complacent in our relationship with God, failing to see His greatness and our lowliness and need for Him, then our inward thoughts about ourselves and our attitudes in relation to others will tend towards pride.

In order to move in the direction of humility, we must

come to the place of real dependence on God. This involves looking at ourselves as vessels which God can fill, and through which He can pour out blessing. We need to see that God is all-important, that the contents matter so much more than the container, and that the latter is only a channel for the streams of living water God wants to pour in. When we are unwilling to be counted as nothing we are still giving too much weight to the container, and unwilling for God to be all.

To desire humility is to desire to be more Christ-like, and it is a desire and longing we need to express daily in prayer. How much do we pray asking God to help us put on humility? We are naturally much more inclined to pray for success and fruitfulness in our ministries than for humility. The secret working of pride in our hearts is often allowed to go on unchallenged. We are, for example, irritated when people pay little attention to us and honour someone else. That is hidden pride. We cannot stand being criticized in front of others. That is hidden pride. We want others to think we are humble. That is hidden pride. We descend into self-pity or withdrawal when our talents or personality are not sufficiently acknowledged. That is hidden pride. All these and countless other expressions of pride can bring stagnation and death to our spiritual lives.

The lack of humility is an explanation for most of our spiritual failures. If we can come to brokenness before God, and lowliness of heart, and be clothed with humility, then we can become empty vessels that God delights to fill with all His goodness and overflowing blessings. We need to pray for humility:

'Please, Lord God, forgive the stirrings of pride in my heart, for seeing myself as better than others. Help me

to live in the Spirit, and teach me humility, and how to put on genuine humility.'

Have you noticed how attractive a truly humble person is? The loveliness of the Holy Spirit shines out with quiet authority. If this is not a contradiction, it is truly a quality to covet!

NOTES TO CHAPTER 5

[1] Isaiah 14:12-14. Isaiah refers in this passage to the deep pride of the king of Babylon. But, behind this taunt against the king, lies the more sinister figure of Satan himself. It is significant that Jesus refers back to this passage in Luke 10:18. 'I saw Satan fall like lightning from heaven.'

[2] See, for example, 1 Samuel 17:47 and Psalm 18:1-3.

[3] See 1 Corinthians 10:12

[4] See 2 Samuel 24:10. The word in Hebrew is 'struck'. David is clearly anxious and full of worry over his sin of pride.

[5] Hezekiah's kingship is described in 2 Kings 18-20.

[6] That both Aaron and Miriam were recognised as leaders, we learn from Micah 6:4. Miriam alone was punished, probably because she took the lead in this protest against Moses.

[7] Murray, Andrew:*Humility: the Beauty of Holiness* , Lakeland, 1961, p.20

Chapter Six

Fear or Faith

THE FOURTH BEAD: FEAR

A person who gets into his car and drives after drinking several glasses of whisky may lose all inhibitions, and may drive at very high speeds without any fear of causing an accident. We can see from this example that not all fear is bad. Indeed, some natural fears are essential to self-preservation and to a healthy society. The fear of having an accident can, on the other hand, become so marked that a person may decide never to get into a car again, or even never to leave the house. This would clearly be an undesirable fear. A fear such as this may even involve a spirit of fear, from which the person in question can be set free through receiving prayer ministry. This would involve first a submission to the Lord Jesus Christ on the part of the afflicted one, followed by a command from the one ministering that the spirit of fear leave, in the name of Jesus Christ. As James writes:

> Submit yourselves, then, to God. Resist the devil, and he will flee from you.
>
> *James 4:7*

For myself, a big fear was that of failure. The root of this probably lay with my father—who was a brilliant man, deeply concerned for my well-being—and with his frustration at my apparent lack of intelligence as a child, particularly in science and mathematics, at which he excelled. His fear that I would fail in life and be a 'good-for-nothing' transferred to me, becoming something I strove to disprove with all my being. I even did a PhD to prove to myself that he was wrong. My wife had a powerful fear of death, due to her father's early death from cancer, a fear which lifted miraculously when she became a Christian. My own fear was dealt with when I came to know myself to be accepted and loved in Christ, and through ministry of the Holy Spirit.

Other people I have known have suffered from fear of flying, elevators, the opinions of others, certain illnesses, financial insecurity, being deserted, and of being found out. It is often possible to find out how an extreme fear took root, then bring it to Jesus and cast it out in his Name. To remain free of fear, we need to embrace faith in the power of God and His good purposes for our lives.

At the very root of fear is the universal fear of death. Whether acknowledged or suppressed, it exercises an influence on all men and women. We do not only shrink in fear from the pain, disease and sorrow that accompany death, but we fear the consequences of the power that lies behind death, namely the power of sin. The Bible teaches us that death is the direct result of sin:

> For the wages of sin is death, but the gift of God is eternal life in Christ Jesus our Lord.
>
> *Romans 6:23*

After death comes judgement [Hebrews 9:27] and, however much this truth is watered down, opposed, ridiculed or suppressed, it will not go away. Our consciences know and fear this prospect. We know we are responsible for our lives, and that one day we must give an account before God. We can never totally suppress this knowledge, and so suffer fear and live with a guilty conscience, unable to break free from the fear of death. Unless we face the truth of the coming judgement, we can never be delivered from the real fear that is there and which influences our behaviour.

The root problem of our fear was dealt with by Jesus on the cross, when he suffered there the penalty for our sin. When a person comes to an understanding of the meaning of Jesus' death, and responds by trusting that Jesus paid the price for his own sin, then he is gloriously set free from the burden of paying for that sin. As he yields his life to Christ, in thanks for Christ's loving sacrifice, he is freed from the fear of death, from the fear of facing God at the coming judgement, for he knows he has been set free from the guilt of his past. He knows that he is now safe in Christ. For such a person, the reign of sin, death and Satan is broken. It is broken on the divine side by the death and resurrection of Jesus Christ, and on the human side by faith in what God has done in Christ.

While the fear of death is the root fear of mankind, there are many other fears which afflict people. Christians may still experience fear, even though the burden of their guilt has been dealt with. They can slip into fear unless they remind themselves that they have been put right with God objectively. The fear that our post-conversion sins have separated us from God is not uncommon. After genuine repentance and faith, a believer may suddenly be plagued by the memory of old sins and feel himself abandoned by God. King David felt like this at times as he reflected on the horror of his past sin of adultery, even though this had already been forgiven by God.

> My guilt has overwhelmed me like a burden too heavy to bear.
>
> *Psalm 38:4*

Fear can be the result of following our own wrong choices. If we break out from the area of God's protection, we may soon encounter fearful situations. For Abraham and David, the Promised Land was that boundary and, as they went beyond it, they became subject to fear, leading Abraham to abandon his wife to Pharaoh's harem, and persuading David to feign madness before the King of Gath.[1] We need to learn from these examples that there are boundaries around us, drawn by God, and if we go beyond these we invite disaster. We need to stay within the boundaries in order to experience the blessings of inner peace. But, even if we do move beyond those boundaries, God is so faithful to us that he yearns for us to return and does not abandon us or leave us to our own resources. In order for us to return to God, though, we must bring our fears into His presence and not try to hide them.

If we expose our fears to God, instead of being ashamed of them and trying to cover them up, we are on the way to victory over fear. The problem is that we do not like admitting our fears and want to appear to others, and even sometimes to God, as if we are perfectly in control. Our natural tendency is to want others to see us as courageous and strong, so we often try to give such an impression. Of course then we can never overcome our inner fears. Fear that is acknowledged is fear that can be defeated; indeed it is the fearful, the weak and helpless who ultimately can become channels for the power of God. But to admit our weakness and fear is only a first step. We must at the same time take hold of the Lord Jesus Christ, trusting in his goodness and power to deliver us and strengthen us to face the situation causing our fear.

There are many Christians who are paralysed in their lives by fear that gnaws away and is allowed to be in control, because that fear has never been brought to God, but remains so hidden and covered up that it is quite a task even to identify it clearly. But if we expose our fears to God, and look to Him as the one who can deliver us, then we will be able to say with David:

> 'I sought the LORD, and he answered me; he delivered me from all my fears. Those who look to him are radiant; their faces are never covered with shame.'
>
> *Psalm 34:4-5*

As we look to the Lord we shall become radiant, reflecting His light and losing all our fears.

KINDS OF FEAR

The fundamental fear, as we have seen, is the fear of death. There is also the basic fear of insecurity, the fear of man, and spiritual fear. The fear of insecurity includes a whole range of circumstances such as looming poverty, unemployment, war, loneliness and disease. This fear of insecurity is a key motivational factor in our society and in nearly all societies. In order to avoid being controlled by the fear of financial insecurity, we must become free from the love of money and must realize that our lives are not basically about the things that we have:

> For the love of money is a root of all kinds of evil. Some people, eager for money, have wandered from the faith and pierced themselves with many griefs.
>
> *1 Timothy 6:10*

Anxiety and fear inevitably go together with the love of money—fear, if one has wealth, of losing it; and fear, if one has little, of poverty and misery. Jesus has given us the answer to this problem — namely contentment, which is a habit of mind that comes through reminding ourselves of God's fatherly provision for us, and His promises:

> So do not worry, saying,"What shall we eat?"or"What shall we drink?"or"What shall we wear?" For the pagans run after all these things, and your heavenly Father knows that you need them. But seek first his kingdom and his righteousness, and all these things will be given to you as well.
>
> *Matthew 6:31-33*

The fear of adverse circumstances such as war, loneliness, unemployment and cancer can have a real grip on our lives. Such fears can be overcome by learning to trust in God's love and in His sovereign control over our lives. Fear goes out of the window when I stand on the truth that God loves me so much that in all things He is working for my good:

> And we know that in all things God works for the good of those who love him, who have been called according to his purpose.
>
> *Romans 8:28*

We can defeat fear as we grow in confidence of the love of God:

> Perfect love drives out fear, because fear has to do with punishment.
>
> *1John 4:18*

Whatever the fear, it should be exposed before God in prayer, and then we should seek His intervention on our behalf. Finally, God should be praised for making the matter His own concern. God wants us to throw off all fear of adverse circumstances, so that we can live by faith and become effective for Him:

> Do not be anxious about anything, but in everything, by prayer and petition, with thanksgiving, present your requests to God. And the peace of God, which transcends all understanding, will guard your hearts and your minds in Christ Jesus.
>
> *Philippians 4:6-7*

The fear of man can be even more invasive in our lives than the fear of adverse circumstances. This fear leads us to make many efforts to please men in order to gain approval—even at the cost of pleasing God. The fear that looks over my shoulder and ponders: 'What do they think of me?'can become a controlling power in my life, causing me to be governed by the need to receive the approval of others. King Saul lost everything in the end, because of the fear of man.

Peer pressure on the Christian young person provokes such fear of man; it is the fear of being thought 'boring' for refusing to go along with an ungodly or immoral course of action. No Christian can become an effective servant of God until he begins to lose this fear of other people, and stops trying to get the approval of others for his actions. Paul is very explicit:

> Am I now trying to win the approval of men, or of God? Or am I trying to please men? If I were still trying to please men, I would not be a servant of Christ.
>
> *Galatians 1:10*

The fear of being misunderstood, ridiculed and rejected can be overcome most effectively by becoming more secure in our relationship with the Lord—to the point where we feel totally secure in Christ. Jesus himself never needed to prove anything. He rested securely in his loving relationship with the Father. So often, we are trying to prove something. This motivational force leads us into fear that we may fail in our efforts. Jesus made himself of no reputation, and so there could be no fear of losing reputation.

As well as the fear of adverse circumstances and the fear of man, there is also what might be termed supernatural fear—or the spirit of fear—which can take a grip. This is the fear which comes directly from a demonic spirit.[2] The spirit of fear may gain entrance to a person through involvement in occult activities, or superstitions, or through a traumatic experience. If the person with the spirit of fear is willing to submit himself to the Lordship of Jesus Christ, the spirit of fear may be cast out in his name.

The Bible speaks very positively of one kind of fear—the fear of the Lord which is the 'beginning of knowledge.'[Proverbs 1:7] It does not mean a craven or cringing fear which sees God as a taskmaster, who watches us to find faults and blemishes and who is just waiting to punish us as a stern and distant law-giver. The biblical fear of the Lord should not terrify us, but make us look up to Him with deep reverence and awe. It involves a hatred of evil, and reverential trust. As we develop this right fear of the Lord, we lose our fear of man and of adverse circumstances.

A good biblical illustration of this right kind of fear was the fear Joseph had of spoiling his relationship with Potiphar, his master—a fear which caused him to resist taking up the urgings of Potiphar's wife that Joseph sleep with her. Joseph was not motivated by a cringing fear of punishment, but by respect for his master and a determination not to sin against God in such a wicked way. A wife who fears to spoil her union with her husband, and who therefore rejects an opportunity for flirtation with another man, does so not because she is frightened of her husband, but because she puts such a high value on her marriage that she treats her husband with true respect. She would not hurt him for anything. A person who would not grieve God is, in the same sense, a person who has the right fear of the Lord.

When we live in such fear of the Lord that we want to do all we can to avoid hurting God, *then* we lose all fear of men. Such a right fear of the Lord will inevitably involve loving others.

ADAM

The first human fear was caused by doubt in Eve's mind about the character of God. Satan both persuaded Eve to doubt God's goodness, by pointing her to God's restrictions placed on herself and Adam, and encouraged her to disbelieve the coming judgement. This is characteristic of all sin—the distortion, and then disbelief, of God's Word (Did God say? —surely not!) Adam wanted to be his own master. But the cost for this self-assertion, and determination to be independent, was a sense of guilt and shame, condemnation and separation from God. As Adam and Eve discovered their nakedness, guilty feelings were aroused and they experienced fear. That which previously had delighted them—the voice of the Lord God—now terrified them. The open, fearless communion Adam had enjoyed with God was now broken. In his 'independence', he now shrinks from God in fear. The wonderful sound of God's voice, which had delighted Adam and Eve, now frightened them.

All the other fears Adam and Eve accumulated, one after the other, derive from their separation from God. As they sought control over their own circumstances without restriction, so they were faced with uncertainty as to how those circumstances might turn out. Before the Fall, those circumstances had been under the sovereign control of God, Adam and Eve having had no basis for any fears. Indeed, they had not known what it was to fear, since the realm in which they lived was totally secure under God's mighty hand. Is there any way we can return to that original security? Only by first admitting and exposing our fears, and by repenting of our desire for autonomy and independence from God; then accepting the only basis for that return—through the blood of Christ by which we can be cleansed of all sin, as we reach out in faith to God. As Adam and Eve were robbed of security, through self-assertion and insistence upon independence from God, so we, their descendants, can conquer fear, recovering security by submission to God; by living under the Lordship of Jesus Christ, and walking in the Spirit—not in the flesh.

ABRAHAM

Abraham, the friend of God, is known above all for his faith; for his willingness to step out in obedience to God's Word. Yet he descended into fear, deserting the path of faith. He did so because he had given way to doubts concerning God's Word. God had brought him into the Promised Land, and had made him quite staggering promises. But, instead of seeing these promises fulfilled, Abraham was faced with famine. The famine was God's 'bread and butter' test and Abraham failed it. He fled from Canaan—without seeking God's guidance. The fear of the prospect of poverty—loss of his flocks and herds, and hunger—drove Abraham to Egypt. He would not trust God to provide for his needs in Canaan, and determined to go from Canaan in order to look after his own needs. He did not believe that God could provide for him in the midst of famine, so the fear of famine made him take matters into his own hands.[3]

Faith brought Abraham to the Promised Land. Fear now caused him to leave it. His problem began with fear, which caused him to give way to doubts about the reliability of God's promises. By giving way to the fear of poverty, Abraham caused suffering for his wife. His fear of famine was followed by the fear that Pharaoh would kill him to get his wife, so Abraham resorted to lies in order to protect himself. He yielded Sarai to Pharaoh, thus endangering the honour of his wife. Abraham's descent into fear led him at once into further sins of selfishness and deception. In effect, he invited the violation of his wife as a means of saving his own skin.

Fear in Adam and Eve, and fear in Abraham, was allowed to take root, because doubts had been sown in their minds about the character of God. The famine shook Abraham's confidence in God's goodness to him, so he grasped at other ways of protecting himself. The words of Satan had caused Eve to consider that perhaps the restriction God had placed on them in the Garden meant that God's goodness was questionable. In both cases there is a downward spiral from doubt to fear, and on to further fears.

THE SPIES

Perhaps the most instructive descent into fear that is recounted in the Bible is the case of the ten spies.[4] Moses appointed representative leaders for each of the twelve tribes, to spy out the land after Israel arrived at Kadesh-Barnea, on the threshold of the Promised Land. In their past history, the Israelites had, time and again, given in to fear—fear of the pursuing Egyptian army, fear of thirst, fear of hunger, fear of enemies. Each time, God had delivered them—revealing His power and love. At Kadesh, the Israelites had reached a crossroads. From this place they were to go in and possess the Promised Land. When the spies returned, they confirmed God's Word concerning the attractiveness and fruitfulness of the land; it was a land 'flowing with milk and honey.' But ten of the spies were overwhelmed by fear of the inhabitants, who were very strong and well-protected. They interpreted the problem entirely on the basis of what they had seen, totally rejecting all the lessons they had been taught concerning the power and love of God. Their fear caused them to magnify and exaggerate the prowess of the Canaanites:

> And they spread among the Israelites a bad report about the land they had explored. They said,"The land we explored devours those living in it. All the people we saw there are of great size."
>
> *Numbers 13:32*

Fear was allowed to control their thinking, to such an extent that it dominated their interpretation of everything that they saw. The difficulties of entering Canaan were so overwhelming, so gigantic, that 'we seemed like grasshoppers...'[Numbers 13:33].

The minority report by Caleb and Joshua was very different, even though they had observed the same scenes as the ten. Caleb interpreted what he observed in the light of his knowledge of God, and of God's promises. Caleb's spirit was yielded to God. He knew that, although the Canaanites were strong, his God was so much mightier—that these giants were just grasshoppers to God. Caleb's faith brought

God into the picture, shutting out fear, whilst the unbelief of the ten meant that they could only depend on sight, thereby effectively excluding God from the situation. Caleb's faith in God caused him to reject the assessment of the ten—that Israel could not prevail against such a powerful enemy.

The report of the ten stirred up the fears of the Israelites, who could easily imagine how fierce, war-like, strongly armed and well-defended were the Canaanite cities. Fear quickly exaggerated the extent of the military task facing the Israelites, so that it came to control their response, persuading them that to go into Canaan would be suicidal. Who could prevail against cities 'with walls up to the sky'?

> "Where can we go? Our brothers have made us lose heart. They say, 'The people are stronger and taller than we are; the cities are large, with walls up to the sky. We even saw the Anakites there.'"
>
> *Deuteronomy 1:28*

The victory of fear and unbelief over faith and obedience proved very costly. For forty years, that generation of Israelites had to wander aimlessly through the desert, only Caleb and Joshua being allowed to enter the Promised Land.

Every Christian has to face his Kadesh-Barnea crisis. This invariably involves being faced with a choice of either remaining in the desert and wandering aimlessly about, or taking a bold step of faith in obeying God's call on his or her life. Fear will be used by Satan to keep believers from moving forward—fear of the conflicts that lie ahead, fear of unpopularity, fear of persecution, fear of poverty, fear of insecurity, fear of what man can do to them. If we allow fear to win in this struggle between the flesh and the Spirit, we shall know only restlessness, and an underlying discontent and preoccupation with self, finding little motivation to fight the battles God has appointed for us.

By refusing to enter the Promised Land, and by rejecting God's purposes for them, the Israelites were refusing to go on in spiritual maturity. It left them depressed, since they had to give up all hope of ever possessing their inheritance. To move forward spiritually, taking the step of faith at our Kadesh-Barnea, does not mean we have to close our eyes to difficulties and the opposition ranged against us. In Scripture, we are never told to deny reality. It is largely a question of interpretation. Fear is not conquered by pretending there are no real difficulties—that the giants are not giants at all—but by approaching the difficulties with faith in the mighty power of God to help and deliver us. The objectively difficult circumstances, the gigantic problems, are interpreted in the light of the Almighty God, who is really there with us, and on whom we can rely for victory.

To conquer fear, we need the attitude of King Jehoshaphat who, when faced with a vast army ranged against Judah, reminded himself of the character and might of Almighty God, and kept his eyes on the Lord:

> Then Jehoshaphat stood up in the assembly of Judah and Jerusalem at the temple of the LORD in the front of the new courtyard and said:"O LORD, God of our fathers, are you not the God who is in heaven? You rule over all the kingdoms of the nations. Power and might are in your hand, and no-one can withstand you.... O our God, will you not judge them? For we have no power to face this vast army that is attacking

us. We do not know what to do, but our eyes are upon you."

2 Chronicles 20: 5-6,12

ELIJAH

Elijah was a man who had been trained, step by step, to trust in God for his every need. When his only supply of water, the stream of Cherith, dried up, Elijah went on trusting God. He learnt the lesson all great men of God have to learn—the lesson of depending on God alone. He learnt the lesson, too, at Zarephath, where God instructed him to seek the help of a poor widow for provision of food. Here, Elijah's faith came into full bloom, with the raising of the widow's dead child. On Mount Carmel, Elijah became the complete servant of the Lord, boldly challenging the false prophets to a contest—to see who is truly God. The Lord sent fire to consume Elijah's sacrifice, and the people returned to the Lord, falling down in worship and crying:'The Lord—he is God'[1 Kings 18:39]. Elijah had the prophets of Baal killed, and prayed for rain to end the drought he had earlier announced. He was now at the very height of his ministry. All the people revered him as the prophet of the Lord, full of power and authority. But this same Elijah, only days later, shrank with fear before the words of Jezebel.

When Ahab told Jezebel, his wife, how the fire from heaven had consumed Elijah's sacrifice, as well as the wood, stones and soil, and how the priests of Baal had been killed, she was furious at the triumph of Elijah. She determined to re-establish her ancestral Baal religion in Israel. She sent a message to Elijah, with this warning: 'May the gods deal with me, be it ever so severely, if by this time tomorrow I do not make your life like that of one of them'[1 Kings 19:2].

Elijah cowers in fear. He shrinks before this woman, running away after having taken on the whole of the political and religious power structure in Israel. However, he is contending not just with one woman, but with the demonic power behind her. Had she not killed God's prophets, and was she not set on wickedness and witchcraft? She, not Ahab, was in control of Israel. This Jezebel foreshadows the Jezebel of the book of Revelation.[5]

Jezebel, and the evil spirit in her, bring fear upon Elijah. Elijah is, indeed, scared off—and what a pathetic sight to see the great prophet running from Jezebel. He is not just up against the wife of Ahab, but against the demonic Jezebel spirit. He descends into fear, because he fails to wait for God's Word in answer to Jezebel's message. He can see only the threat to himself. He takes his eyes off God and is absorbed with himself and so '...was afraid and ran for his life'[1 Kings 19:3a].

He was running now—not for God, but for his life; for himself. When Elijah stands there without a word from God, he is just like any other man. No-one, not even Elijah, is anything without the Lord. How quickly Elijah came down from his Carmel mountain-top experience, into the desert. He is driven by fear, self-pity and loss of vision. Yet, how wonderful are God's dealings with Elijah in his depression. God is touched by his weaknesses and failures, consoling him and building him up. Here is confirmation that God does not love us less when we fail. God did not love Elijah more on Mount Carmel than when he ran away from

Jezebel. It is the same with us. God's love for us never changes, only our awareness of it changes. We can come out of fear and back into faith and security, when we stop running for self and return to running for God.

One of the ways in which fear is generated in believers is through the notion that they need to succeed in order to be loved. The pastor, for example, fears that he will not be loved unless he preaches well, visits conscientiously and counsels successfully. The evangelist fears that he will not be loved unless there is a good response to his call for conversions. The child fears he will not be loved unless he excels at school, in sport, or some artistic field. The woman fears she will not be loved unless she retains her youthful looks or has a beautiful home. The man fears he will not be loved if he loses his job and so his ability to make material provision. All these fears are related to performance: 'If I perform well, I will be loved—or at least love will not be withdrawn from me.'

While it is good and proper for all tasks to be done conscientiously, the nature of our Christian fellowship with one another will be adversely affected if there is a hidden motive of fear of failure underlying our performances. First, we must ensure that our relationship with God is free of a wrong, cringing fear. We must know in our hearts that we can never earn God's love, but that it is given unconditionally to those who are in Christ, and that, when we fail at anything, Christ loves us no less than when we succeed. We need to know that we are loved by God simply because we are His children. Then we can rejoice in the freedom of realizing the security of His steadfast love. Fear is banished as I walk in the security of God's love, knowing that this love depends not on my doings, but on His character.

In our relationships within the body of Christ, the church, we need to learn to see one another as members who belong, and are loved, not for what we do—the particular functions we perform—but simply for who we are as brothers and sisters in Christ. Just as we must cease trying to earn God's love, so we should cease trying to earn the love of fellow members. The struggle against fear is the struggle to believe that I am loved because of who I am in Christ, rather than because of what I do. This aspect of the struggle involves disconnecting love from rewards.

STORMS

The example of Peter stepping out of the boat on the Sea of Galilee, in response to the invitation of Jesus to come to him, teaches us much about the relationship between fear and faith. The other apostles must have been amazed at the courage of Peter, as he lowered himself over the side of the boat, then walked on the surging water. He began to sink because he began to look at the waves, instead of keeping his gaze fixed on Jesus. The problem was not that the storm came after Peter's initial step of faith out onto the water. The storm had begun even before Jesus came anywhere near the boat. Peter's faith began to weaken at the close-up view of the danger he was in, and as his faith ebbed away he began to sink. He was sinking because fear was driving away faith. Without faith, Peter had lost access to the upholding power of Christ. Jesus was holding Peter up because of the trust Peter had in his power. As Peter gave way to fear, losing faith in Christ's power to hold him up, he began to sink. There is an important principle here—namely that Christ's power for us is exercised on condition of our faith. As soon as we lose faith, as our trust in Christ is given up; as soon as fear begins to gain the upper hand and control our behaviour, then the influence of Christ's power into our lives diminishes. Peter walked on the waves as if on a solid path *as long as he believed.* As soon as he stopped believing and was filled with fear, he began to sink.

Peter was shaken with fear, because his trust in Jesus was still weak and he was full of doubts. Similarly, we give way to fears because our faith is weak and we are subject to doubts. Strong faith focusses on the person of Jesus, not on the waves—not on the difficulties we are encountering. Strong faith says: '...he who began a good work in you will carry it on to completion...'[Philippians 1:6]; and,'...the one who is in you is greater than the one who is in the world' [1 John 4:4].

Christ holds us up when we trust him. Fear comes in to contend with faith, seeking to dislodge the believer from walking by faith in Christ. Satan seeks to get us to look away from Christ and to occupy our thoughts with dangers and obstacles. If he succeeds in shifting our focus in this way, he is winning. Such a shift invariably strengthens doubts, leading to the collapse of faith and the reign of fear. But the reign of fear can be broken if, through that very fear, we are thrown back onto the Lord.

It was the fear of death which broke Peter's faith, causing terror in his heart, so that he began to sink: but then, in the midst of the dangers, Peter's initial faith was rekindled—he cried out to the Lord, 'save me'. The very difficulties and dangers in our lives which draw us into doubts and fear can, as we get immersed in them, also cause us to emerge with renewed faith—crying out to our God for deliverance and help, so that we throw ourselves back again into dependence on Him. As Peter cried out in fear, the Lord stretched forth His hand to save and restore him. How often this scene has been repeated in the life of every Christian. The grace of God is such that He rescues us from our own fears, which we caused by letting our eyes stray from Him onto our problems and difficulties.

In the episode in which the disciples are caught in a storm on the Sea of Galilee with Jesus asleep in the boat, we again can see how fear stifles the disciples' faith. They had seen Jesus do remarkable things and certainly believed in him. They knew in their minds that God's plan through Christ would not be allowed to founder because of a sudden storm. But fear is such a strong emotion that it pushes faith and reason away. It is constantly used by Satan to encourage God's people to fall into unbelief. By contrast, God often exhorts us in His Word to put away fear, and instead to trust in His power.

After calming the storm on the Sea of Galilee, Jesus says to his disciples:'...Why are you so afraid? Do you still have no faith?'[Mark 4:40] Here we see clearly that, in a spiritual sense, fear and faith are opposites. Fear is the response of the flesh. Faith is the response of the promptings of the Spirit. The fruit of the Spirit is faith, whereas the work of the flesh is fear. Jesus showed that the disciples had given way to fear because they were deficient in faith. If we have a problem with fear in our lives, it is really a problem with faith. The way to become free of fear is to become full of faith—faith in the power and goodness of Christ.

FIGHTING FEAR WITH FAITH

A factor underlying fear can be a reluctance to die to self. Self-love, self-concern, self-pity, and self-protection all feed fear. The person who is full of fears is nearly always a person who is self-absorbed, rather than focussed on God and on other people. When we are living by the Spirit, we are enabled to love God and to become involved in the lives of others and so give fewer opportunities for fear to flourish because, 'perfect love drives out fear'[1 John 4:18]. The confidence we have in God as our Father, and the intimacy and depth of His love for us, help to remove fear from our hearts. Assurance of salvation—knowing that we belong to God, because of Jesus' death on the cross for us personally—means that, despite all we can still see in ourselves that is not good, ultimately there is nothing to fear. Assurance of God's favour towards us in this life, knowing He has a plan for our lives that is good and wholesome, should give Christians confidence and trust which can dispel every fear.

When we believe the Word of God with all our hearts, fear is driven away. Who can remain in fear, and be controlled by fear, when taking into himself, into his inner being, the words of Romans 8:28 that, 'We know that in all things God works for the good of those who love him, who have been called according to his purpose.'

Concerning the anxieties and fears likely to take hold on a day to day basis, I have found it very helpful to come to the Lord as soon as the first feelings of fear stir in my heart, to acknowledge them, then ask for faith in Christ to replace the fear.

'Please Lord, I am afraid, but I want to trust you and

see this as an opportunity for putting my trust in You. I ask you to strengthen my faith and deliver me from this fear.'

Think of the Lord's love for you, His promises, and past deliverance from fear. Bring to mind scriptures that stress God's faithfulness. Place yourself at the centre of God's will for your life. Praise Him for His good purposes for you.

NOTES TO CHAPTER 6

[1] These episodes are recounted in Genesis 12:10-20 and in 1 Samuel 21:10-15

[2] Scriptural references to a spirit of fear occur in Romans 8:15; 2 Timothy 1:7 and Job 4:14,15

[3] See Genesis 12:10-20. Exactly the same circumstance is the background for the book of Ruth. Ruth's husband sets out with his family to leave Israel to escape famine conditions—fear drives him to leave. God redeems the situation wonderfully through Ruth's faith.

[4] The account is recorded in Number 13-14

[5] See Revelation 2:20-24. There is a further indirect reference to a harlot spirit in Revelation 18:7-8, identified as Babylon. Here is the consummation of the system of evil, in the woman who sits on the scarlet beast.

Chapter Seven

Loudmouthedness, or Gentleness and Self-Control

THE FIFTH BEAD OF LOUDMOUTHEDNESS

I am sure this was one of my beads because the Lord saw it as one of my most besetting sins. I grew up in an atmosphere where to speak bluntly, openly express feelings, and hold passionate views was considered normal and admirable. Whilst these are not necessarily negative values, in my case they led to a tendency to be aggressive and insensitive to others, and to adopt an arrogant tone. My having spent some years as an academic, during which arguing, debating and point-scoring was a normal part of life, only encouraged this trait in my character. The Lord showed me that He wanted all this to change. He wanted me to become gentle where I had been harsh, and this has been one of my most challenging struggles. In the natural, I would blurt out exactly what I thought, often giving way to anger. In the Spirit, the Lord is continuing to help me to surrender my reactions, words and tone of voice to His guidance. I have found it helpful to pray, often with my wife, specifically for help, when I think I may face a difficult meeting or interview, that my reactions would come under the control of the Holy Spirit.

'Loudmouthedness', not a word you would find in a dictionary, is the tendency to speak without restraint in numerous situations; to express verbally feelings and thoughts about a particular circumstance or person without much reflection, and certainly without submitting those thoughts and feelings to the Holy Spirit. It is the fleshly tendency to open one's mouth and speak in such a way that God is not glorified, others are hurt or discouraged, and the self is lifted up.

The Bible leaves us in no doubt that our words are important—not least because they are a reliable indicator of our inner life. It is through our words that the state of our hearts is often revealed. As Jesus put it:-

> '...For out of the overflow of the heart the mouth speaks. The good man brings good things out of the good stored up in him, and the evil man brings evil things out of the evil, stored up in him. But I tell you that men will have to give account on the day of judgement for every careless word they have spoken. For by your words you will be acquitted, and by your words you will be condemned.'
>
> *Matthew 12:34b-37*

Jesus does not allow us to detract from the importance of words with the speculation that deeds are just far more expressive of character than words. Men, not God, make such distinctions. What comes from a man's mouth is a self-revelation. No excuse can break the connection between the heart and the mouth. The general tenor of our thoughts and will are going to be revealed by our speech. The link between the heart and the mouth is brilliantly captured by Paul in these words:

> For it is with your heart that you believe and are justified, and it is with your mouth that you confess and are saved.
>
> *Romans 10:10*

Our salvation depends both on exercising faith in our hearts and on making the appropriate confession with our mouths. Just as a cistern which is too full flows into an overflow pipe, so what is in the heart will flow out through the mouth. It is as if the heart employs the mouth as its channel for outward expression. The idle and innocuous word spontaneously spoken out without prior consideration may well reveal what is kept in the storehouse of our hearts. To remonstrate 'I did not mean it' after a lightly spoken word is really beside the point, since one's true disposition is often revealed by just such words. In any case, Jesus tells us that we shall be held responsible for silly chatter and purposeless speech and have to give account. He is adamant that words spoken from an impure heart make a man unclean. No excuse can break the connection between our words and our character.

When the prophet Isaiah was given a vision of the glory of God, he was immediately made conscious of his sin by becoming aware of his unclean lips. Failure in the area of the tongue is as significant as failure in actions:

> "Woe to me!" I cried."I am ruined! For I am a man of unclean lips, and I live among a people of unclean

> lips, and my eyes have seen the King, the LORD Almighty." Then one of the seraphs flew to me with a live coal in his hand, which he had taken with tongs from the altar. With it he touched my mouth and said, "See, this has touched your lips; your guilt is taken away and your sin atoned for."
>
> *Isaiah 6:5-7*

In his vision, Isaiah is burdened by the consciousness of his unclean lips, but his guilt is burnt away by one of the seraphim. From God's point of view, all people have unclean lips. Every person needs forgiveness for the sins of the tongue, so when, in Romans chapter three, Paul describes the universal sinfulness of mankind, he includes sins of speech.

The potential for evil from our mouths can hardly be exaggerated. Untold harm is done through careless, hasty, bitter words which work their poison through whole fellowships, hindering God's work in the community. That something as small and apparently insignificant as the tongue can have decisive influence, is demonstrated by James in three successive pictures: the horse's bit, the ship's rudder, and the spark.[1] A horse, no matter how strong it might be, can be brought under control by a small piece of metal in its mouth. Likewise, a person whose tongue is properly tamed is in control of his or her whole being. The rudder of a great ocean liner is just a tiny part of the ship but, as the ship's helmsman turns it, the whole course of the ship is determined. Similarly, the human tongue may greatly influence the course of a person's life. James goes on to compare the tongue to a tiny spark that can do an enormous amount of damage by setting a whole forest ablaze, destroying something that is beautiful and useful. Once the damage is done, that particular forest is gone forever. How many beautiful and useful relationships or reputations have been destroyed by unwise speech: unity can be shattered, a reputation damaged, a friendship spoiled, a work of God hindered.

It is in this matter of the tongue that the battle between the flesh and the Spirit is so frequently lost in the life of the believer. We find ourselves defeated, because control over the tongue, apart from the Spirit, is impossible. As James puts it:

> We all stumble in many ways. If anyone is never at fault in what he says, he is a perfect man, able to keep his whole body in check.... All kinds of animals, birds, reptiles and creatures of the sea are being tamed and have been tamed by man, but no man can tame the tongue. It is a restless evil, full of deadly poison.
>
> *James 3:2,7-8*

There is a restless power associated with the tongue, which can hinder our progress into maturity and the Spirit-filled life. We can never claim that we have won complete victory over the tongue and relax, because it always threatens to break any bounds that have been set for it.

The failure by Moses to hesitate and think before speaking on one occasion, is a good reminder of the need to be vigilant—even for the most mature and godly of people. Moses' failure on that one occasion kept him outside the Promised Land. His outburst determined the course of his last years of life. Moses, whose humility and self-acknowledged inarticulateness had marked his first conversation with God, was goaded by the endless grumbling of the Israelites to lash out with his tongue and speak rashly. He lost his temper, striking the rock at Meribah, instead of speaking to it as God had commanded:

> By the waters of Meribah they angered the LORD, and trouble came to Moses because of them; for they rebelled against the Spirit of God, and rash words came from Moses' lips.[2]

This is the only recorded occasion on which Moses was hasty and ungodly with his tongue. But it was enough to rob him of the joy of bringing his mission to a conclusion. We too can easily lose the spiritual blessing God has planned for us by allowing ourselves to be provoked into speaking too hastily.

MANIFESTATIONS OF LOUDMOUTHEDNESS: GRUMBLING

Perhaps the most widespread sin of the tongue is the sin of complaining and grumbling about our circumstances. The history of the Exodus makes a good object lesson. The Israelites complained at virtually every disappointment or problem on their way. Only a few days after the miraculous deliverance through the Red Sea, and after singing the joyful words: 'The Lord is my strength and my song; he has become my salvation'[Exodus 15:2], they grumbled at finding the water at Marah bitter and undrinkable. Their disappointment led them to blame Moses, forgetting they had been led to that place by the pillar of cloud—in other words, by the Lord Himself. Their grumbling at Moses was really a murmuring against God. God graciously overlooked their murmurings, showing Moses how to sweeten the water. Soon they started grumbling again, this time at the lack of food—showing total lack of faith in God, and His ability to feed them in the desert. This provides a salutary reminder that our complaints and murmurings are really against God, since He is the one in sovereign control of the lives of His people. Just as surely as the Israelites were directed by the pillar of cloud, so those in Christ are led by the Holy Spirit, only facing those circumstances which are permitted by Him.

Despite their grumbling, and their having forgotten their deliverance from slavery, God in His great mercy provided them with food through the miracle of the manna. But no sooner had their hunger been satisfied, than they complained again about lack of water. God had done everything for His people. He had saved them from the Egyptians, guided and protected them with His own presence in the pillar of cloud, provided food and water—but in the face of a new need they promptly forgot all that God had already done for them. What a picture this is of our own tendency to forget to trust God continually. How often have I failed to keep my eyes on Christ, forgotten his past mercies and provision, and given way to grumbling about a difficult situation I faced. Again, in amazing mercy and kindness, God provided the Israelites with water at Rephidim, in spite of their forgetfulness.

The fact that the miracles of guidance and provision, over a period of two years, had made no deep impression on Israel, becomes clear from their response to the report of the spies sent out to reconnoitre the promised land of Canaan. As we have seen, they all agreed that Canaan was a good and fertile land, but ten of them aroused such fear and worry in the whole community that the Israelites forgot God's promises. They began to cry out 'back to Egypt,'and were even ready to put on the old chains of slavery. This shows that repeated grumbling can lead to rebelliousness, which may in turn lead to a departure from God's perfect plan, and a return to the old slavery. It is fascinating to consider how the very words they spoke would decide their future. The majority declared that they would not be able to enter and conquer the land. Because of their very words, they were indeed unable to do so, ultimately failing to receive God's promise. The minority of two (Caleb and Joshua) declared with confidence that they would be able to go up and conquer the land, wanting to go in straight away. They were, in fact, the only men of their generation who survived, and did indeed go up and conquer the land. The very words they spoke decided their future. We should never say that words are unimportant. Words of doubt and unbelief can hold us back and bring spiritual death, while words of faith and trust in the power of our God are words which impart life and open doors which would otherwise remain closed. There is great power in the tongue for good, as well as for bad.

Writing in 1 Corinthians 10, Paul takes the history of Israel's grumbling against God as a warning to Christians. It is a warning to us, because we will have the same temptations to complain in a rebellious spirit when we become weary, or consider our God-given tasks too hard. Grumbling encouraged a spirit of rebellion and insubordination, which led some of the Corinthians to challenge their spiritual leaders, bringing the church into considerable disorder. The failure and collapse of Israel on their journey to the Promised Land is a failure we can repeat by muttering and murmuring against our circumstances, in such a way that we are stumbling into unbelief.

One of the clearest illustrations of grumbling in the New Testament is given by Jesus in his parable of the Workers in the Vineyard.[3] The parable describes how an employer offers work at different times of day to the unemployed, some working all day for an agreed hourly wage, others working for part of the day, while others work for only one hour. All workers received the same pay. Those who had worked longest became embittered. They became angry with the boss, accusing him of injustice. Their labour contract had been perfectly honoured. They understood that. What they could not understand and accept was that the boss was entitled to hand out bonuses to the others. They grumbled at his generosity. Here we come to the real root meaning of *gonguzo* (grumble).[4]

The grumblers in the vineyard refused to interpret the owner's attitude to the last workers as good and generous, and are therefore also unable to see that their own contract with him, for service, was really a gift. He could have left them all standing in the market place, unemployed. The generosity of the boss is interpreted as injustice. When we grumble, we show we are incapable of recognising the goodness and generosity of God. It reveals an ungodly attitude that can go beyond dissatisfaction at unfulfilled hopes to the point of accusing God of unfairness. Far from admiring the boundless goodness of God, it may be wrongly decried as unjust. To grumble against one's situation is to accuse God of injustice. It is an insult to God, denigrating His character, and that is why this particular sin of the tongue is dealt with severely.

GOSSIPING AND DEFAMING

Gossiping is described as follows in the Book of Proverbs:

> Without wood a fire goes out; without gossip a quarrel dies down.
>
> *Proverbs 26:20*

> The words of a gossip are like choice morsels; they go down to a man's inmost parts.
>
> *Proverbs 26:22*

The attitude of one person toward another may be deeply affected by a mere whisper. The words spoken into the ear, not necessarily maliciously, but spoken simply by a loose tongue, can do incalculable harm—as much harm as words spoken by a bitter tongue. Words implant ideas in the mind of the hearer, independently of the motives held by the person speaking those words. This is precisely why it is so crucially important for Christians to control their tongues, and to avoid speaking loosely and negatively about others, refusing to listen to any such talk, either passively or actively. It is a fact that people frequently find pleasure in repeating, and magnifying, negative news about others, whilst being quite unaware of bearing them any ill-will.

One of the reasons gossip is such a problem in many churches is that it is not considered to be as serious a sin as it really is. A person who would not dream of stealing or committing adultery may hardly hesitate to repeat some information about a brother or sister—talk which could do immense damage to that person.

To go round spreading idle, untrue or exaggerated details

about another is both to accuse them, and to allow oneself to be used by Satan. This is because, in all of us, there is that fleshly tendency to rejoice when we hear something negative about someone else, so we can easily be drawn in. This tendency is a feature of the fleshly nature, springing from deep roots of jealousy and pride. Through passing on critical words about others, even if this is not motivated by conscious malice, we reflect credit on ourselves through an assumed personal freedom from the fault or weakness in question.

Gossip is evil, because through it we can elevate ourselves by casting down another. It is really a subtle way of expressing our pride. For example, someone may say: 'Of course, John's problem is that he has no sense of money. It just runs through his fingers like water. He just has no idea of budgeting.' This may well come from the heart of one who prides himself on the virtues of good, sound financial management. Someone else may say: 'No wonder those children behave so badly; they are never disciplined at home.' Here, there is pride in the speaker—that *his* children behave well, and are disciplined at home. Words which we have implanted in people's minds cannot be dug out. These words are now a part of the thinking of those who listened to us, though they can be forgiven where there is repentance at the foot of the cross.

Paul aptly refers to 'biting and devouring each other'[Galatians 5:15], and this inhibits the development of a genuine fellowship, based on trust and mutual reliance. If I feel I am being gossiped about, I cease to trust the one whom I suspect, withdrawing myself from him. The fear of being devoured prevents true communication. The moment gossip begins to prevail in a church, a measure of light is extinguished. Darkness establishes itself.

LYING

The Bible leaves us in no doubt that God hates lies:

> The Lord detests lying lips, but he delights in men who are truthful.
>
> *Proverbs 12:22*

There is no grey area between that which is truth and that which is lies, so that all that is not truthful is lies. An exaggeration, which is used in order to bolster one's own reputation in some way, is really a lie, displeasing God. When we yield to the temptation to exaggerate our own merits or achievements, we are really yielding to the temptation to tell lies, even though we may feel more comfortable to think of it as harmless exaggeration.

The very first sin of man resulted from a lie whispered into the ear of Eve by Satan, concerning the character and being of God. The reason God detests lying is that Jesus himself is the Truth, and the Holy Spirit is the Spirit of Truth, whilst Satan is the father of lies. To lie is to be exactly opposite to the character of God, and it is to allow Satan on to your tongue. Jesus denounced Satan as the father of lies:

> "He [the Devil] was a murderer from the beginning, not holding to the truth, for there is no truth in him. When he lies, he speaks his native language, for he is a liar and the father of lies."
>
> *John 8:44b*

One of the early signs of someone who has been genuinely converted is their attempt to step out of the world of deceit, into truthfulness. Our consciences are enlivened by the Holy Spirit, and we start to care about truth and honesty. I recall being challenged about my tax return, and the need to get it right. A man I knew felt constrained to return supplies that had been taken home from his office. Another sent back to the library books he had taken. It is a constant challenge to me not to make exaggerated claims about successes.

As if to confirm that heaven will have no room for any falsehood, we read in the last chapter of the Bible:

> Blessed are those who wash their robes, that they may have the right to the tree of life and may go through the gates into the city. Outside are the dogs, those who practise magic arts, the sexually immoral, the murderers, the idolaters and everyone who loves and practises falsehood.
>
> *Revelation 22:14-15*

BOASTING AND FLATTERY

Showing-off, talking big, and any self-display, are all expressions of pride and arrogance. The proud man uses words to make himself sound clever and witty. He wants to be set apart from his fellows. Boasting reveals a self-confidence inappropriate for a believer who knows that he is dependent on God and ought not to be ashamed to acknowledge that dependence. Boasting can easily creep in as a result of excessive talking. It is as if the greater the number of words spoken, the more difficult it is to avoid falling into a trap of self-exaltation. Proverbs expresses it like this:-

> When words are many, sin is not absent, but he who holds his tongue is wise.
>
> *Proverbs 10:19*

Excessive speaking may also be indicative of inner agitation and lack of peace. It leads to empty talk, boasting and sometimes flattery. Flattery is not always just using words deceitfully to give pleasure, but is often motivated by self-interest. A person may be flattered in order to prepare him to validate some course of action being planned by the flatterer.

> Whoever flatters his neighbour is spreading a net for his feet.
>
> *Proverbs 29:5*

If, on the other hand, one is tempted to engage in flattery oneself, the warning of Scripture is no less severe:

> May the Lord cut off all flattering lips and every boastful tongue....
>
> *Psalm 12:3*

SHOUTING AND BLAMING

Passionate rage is an emotion, and the easy loss of temper is a disposition, which some believe to be invincible. They find themselves giving way to their tongues at some unexpected provocation. Some people can get easily excited and raise their voices in a quarrel, then start shouting—and, in extreme cases, shrieking with rage. Something, which may begin with an indignant outburst, can accelerate with shouting and seething fury. For those who complain of difficulty in controlling their temper, the slightest spark may be enough to set them alight. The person who, to all outward appearances, is respectable, serving the Lord with enthusiasm—apparently fruitful—may be quite different in his home. Behind closed doors there may be outbursts of anger and shouting which would surprise his friends. His family may have had to live with these manifestations for many years. His wife may be in danger of being crushed by repeated outbursts of shouting and apparently uncontrollable loss of temper. Such rage and shouting is a manifestation of the flesh, which the Lord dealt with in my own life.

In order to be rid of the sin of anger, I found that it was helpful to recognize that loss of temper and shouting often began when, in the moment of crisis and under real pressure of inward or outward stress, I found someone else to blame.

This propensity to blame others began straight after the Fall, with Adam first blaming Eve, then God for giving him Eve! It is part of our fallen human nature that in our moments of crisis, when we fail, we immediately look for someone else to blame. We all have this fleshly tendency to blame others for our failures—whether we blame God, Satan or someone else. Quickly, as a kind of inbuilt sinful response, we blame others, finding it so hard to say: 'I am to blame; it is my fault, and I am guilty.'

Blaming others, and a spirit of censoriousness—a critical spirit that finds it difficult to praise others, but very easy to apportion blame—is a common failing. It hinders the development of genuine Christian love and unity, whether in a marriage or a church fellowship. If we are to become free of the readiness to blame others, we shall need to be able to recognize our own failure to respond well to difficult situations.

VICTORY OVER LOUDMOUTHEDNESS: JUDGING BRINGS JUDGEMENT

The root of the problem of the tongue is in the heart. As we have seen, the words which come out of the mouth indicate the condition of the heart. Whatever overflows into—and then comes out of—our mouths, has issued forth from the heart. Any victory we may be able to have in the area of our tongues must be a victory that is at the level of the heart—i.e. of the inner being, the mind and will. If there is a root attitude of fault-finding in my heart, a negative critical spirit, then it will manifest itself in the way I speak. Even though I may have the objective of being kind and positive in what I say, my words will be poisoned by this root in my heart of judgmentalism, and much of what comes out of my mouth will be negative.

If we obeyed the command of Jesus to 'judge not', much of our verbal communication would be transformed. Certainly, we would be far less inclined to gossip, to lie, to shout and blame. Behind the judgmental spirit, which condemns others, is an expectation of finding faults in people, and a tendency to be disappointed if they are not discovered. Jesus warns against this harsh and destructive judgement of others' failings. In the parable of the speck and the plank in Matthew chapter seven, he exposes the perversity of judging others. We can easily condemn, in others, the weaknesses we dare not face up to in ourselves.

Jesus discourages us from judging others, by revealing that in doing so we expose ourselves to the judgement of God.

How good it would be if we could remind ourselves of this inevitable penalty of fault-finding and gossiping. God is not going to wink at our sins of the mouth. Judging a brother or sister in Christ negatively will bring us into the fearful prospect of God's judgement. Let us remember to bite our tongues, rather than fall into the trap of fault-finding, with all its consequences for us.

A wonderful example of restraint in the whole matter of judging one's brother was John Hyde, known also as Praying Hyde, and as the Apostle of Prayer. He describes an incident in his life, which taught him to be very cautious in this area. Deeply burdened by the spiritual condition of a certain pastor, he began to intercede for him like this:

> "O Father, thou knowest how cold —" But a finger seemed to be laid on his lips, so that the word was not uttered and a voice said in his ear, "he that toucheth him, toucheth the apple of Mine eye." Mr. Hyde cried out in sorrow: "Forgive me, Father, in that I have been an accuser of the brethren before Thee!..." then John asked the Father to show him all that was to be praised... in that pastor's life. He was reminded of much for which he could heartily thank God, and spent his time in praise! This was the way to victory. The result? He shortly afterwards heard that the pastor had that very time received a great reviving and was preaching with fire.[5]

It is the condition of our hearts which determines what will come from our mouths. If we have a pure heart, we will have a pure tongue. If we have a non-judgmental, non-condemning heart, but an open accepting heart, then we shall not give way to the temptation to engage in gossip, blaming others for our own shortcomings. The greatest protection for our tongues will be the protection of our hearts from all evil:

> Above all else guard your heart, for it is the wellspring of life.
>
> *Proverbs 4:23*

GENTLENESS AND SELF-CONTROL: FRUIT OF THE HOLY SPIRIT

We have already learned from James that the tongue cannot be tamed. We should recognize that we cannot control our own tongues, however great our determination and self-exertion. They can only be controlled by coming under the control of the Holy Spirit. This means not only refusing to use the tongue for sinful purposes, but more than this—yielding it to God as an instrument of righteousness. Unless the tongue is so yielded to God the Holy Spirit, it will soon slip back into old ways. There is no neutral ground, which might enable one to reject the temptation of misuse without the Holy Spirit. If sin is to be avoided, then the tongue must be available to the Holy Spirit to be used for positive purposes. It is not possible simply to avoid sinful speech. Unless one's mouth is yielded to God, to be used positively for His purposes, it will soon revert to negative expressions—however strong our will. The positive purpose for which God gave us speech was that we might bring glory to His name with our lips. When we yield ourselves to the Holy Spirit, obeying the command to be filled with the Holy Spirit, we will be released—not just to abstain from speaking evil, but to pour out what is good and wholesome.

Instead of grumbling, swearing, lying, boasting, spreading gossip, shouting and blaming others, the one who is full of the Holy Spirit uses his mouth positively to bring glory to God. When the Holy Spirit fills a person, he brings that person's tongue under his control so that what comes out of the mouth is positive. There will no longer be grumbling, but rather praising God. There will be words of encouragement and edification, words that bring healing and unity. Since the Holy Spirit is the Spirit of Truth, there will be no longer lies or slander, but rather a clinging to the truth.

There is only one way to avoid falling into one of the many sins of the tongue and that is by first confessing our own powerlessness to exercise control over our tongue, and then by yielding it up to God for His control, and by being filled with the Holy Spirit. Only by being filled with the Holy Spirit can we be sure that what is coming from our hearts onto our tongues is a positive rather than negative overflow. It can be helpful to decide to become an encourager.

It is significant that at Pentecost, when the disciples were filled with the Holy Spirit, their tongues were wonderfully transformed. Not only were they given new languages to praise God, 'to declare the wonders of God', but Peter was empowered to preach the Gospel—to speak the words of the Gospel, which brought three thousand people to faith and great glory to God.

NOTES TO CHAPTER 7

[1] James 3:3-6

[2] See Psalm 106:32-33. See also the details in Numbers 20:1-13

[3] See Matthew 20:1-16

[4] This is the onomatopoeic Greek word which means to murmur, grumble, mutter.

[5] McGaw, F. *Praying Hyde*, Bethany, Minneapolis, 1970, pp.52-53.

Chapter Eight

A Renewed Relationship

In the struggle between flesh and Spirit, neutrality is impossible. We must either follow the flesh or live according to the Spirit. There can be no middle way. If we ignore the promptings of the Spirit, we will inevitably bring forth concrete works of the flesh. Jealousy, for example, leads to lack of peace, broken relationships and stress, whilst compassion leads to peace of mind, encouragement, unity and well-being.

Because the desires of flesh and Spirit are so diametrically opposed to each other, and because all believers have both the old and the new natures within them, there is inevitable ongoing warfare, which seems very fierce at times, during this earthly life. Whilst there is a state of tension in which we necessarily stand, possessing as we do these two natures, this does not mean that we need to be in a state of uncertainty or irresolution. We can choose either to live according to the old nature by the flesh, or to live according to the new nature by the Holy Spirit. If we choose the former, we will soon become frustrated. We will then be aware of being spiritually defeated and feel distant from our new master, Christ. If we choose to walk by the Spirit, though this may involve many difficulties and even suffering, we will experience an inner peace and joy, and the kind of relationship with the Lord that He planned all along, as well as a transformed life. We will become aware that we are living for the purpose for which we were created and redeemed. In submitting to the control and guidance of the Holy Spirit, we are really saying 'Yes' to our new master, Christ, and 'No' to our previous master, Sin.

The flesh strives to prevent Spirit-inspired desire coming to the fore, and sometimes it seems as though the believer is torn apart by conflicting desires within. If we allow the very conflict to oppress us, however, we are not, as it were, on neutral ground, but are indulging in the flesh. In Romans 7:14-25, Paul describes this oppressive tension between the flesh and Spirit within. He is writing from the perspective of one who is experiencing such a struggle because the flesh rather than the Spirit is being accommodated. When we give way to the flesh, whilst being aware of the promptings of the Holy Spirit within, we will experience unbearable tensions of the kind Paul describes. But we have the option of living by the Spirit. As soon as this choice is made, and the old fleshly way abandoned, then there is a tremendous resolution—a victory won. The earlier cry of frustration becomes a song of peace. The state of tension lasts only as long as we yield to the desires of the flesh. The essence of Christian discipleship is putting off the works of the flesh and living by the Spirit in such a way that he—the Holy Spirit—brings forth fruit in our lives, so that we increasingly become the people God intended us to be, fully able to worship and please Him.

Consider a specific example. When I feel jealous of another, I find it hard to love that person and to be at peace with the Lord. The Holy Spirit prompts me to lay aside this jealousy and to be kind to the person in question. For a time, I might struggle on account of this prompting. It is as though there is a war within me, between the promptings of the Spirit and my human nature. However, while this war is going on, I continue to give way to jealousy and feel deeply frustrated. As soon as I lay down my jealous feelings (and this is usually a matter of the will), I find that my attitude has completely changed. Then I feel compassion for the person. The promptings of the Holy Spirit have been heeded, and now the Spirit begins to bring forth in me the fruit of love, joy, peace.

The outcome of the struggle between flesh and Spirit will depend on several factors. Are we, as believers, aware that such a struggle is actually proceeding within, and that there are two dimensions to our lives that run counter to each other and are in conflict? Unawareness of this struggle gives a considerable advantage to the flesh. The process of self-justification will be difficult to resist if such ignorance prevails. Are our minds being renewed, so that we are thinking more and more in a biblical way about all areas of our lives, or are there certain strongholds of the enemy over our minds that are not yet identified and breached? Do we understand what Paul means in Romans chapter six, about being dead to sin? Do we reckon ourselves dead to sin, knowing that the old master, Sin, no longer has any rights over us? Have we really understood that there is nothing good about the flesh, or do we think about it in such a way that we have not yet learned to hate the flesh, regarding it as that dimension of our being through which we can lose our crown?

In this book I have focussed on the fleshly sins of the mind—on jealousy, covetousness, pride, fear and loudmouthedness, rather than the sins of the body. The challenge for each of us is to discern those areas in our lives that have become strongholds from which we need to be freed, and then to receive an opposite spiritual quality. Some of us are choked by such things as judgementalism, anger, lust and sexual immorality, criticism, untruthfulness, love of money, resentment, bitterness or unforgiveness. The Lord wants to set us free so that we become worthy temples of the Holy Spirit, living to love and praise Him, and for the encouragement and benefit of others.

May I suggest four helpful pointers in gaining victory:

1. Repent of each sinful attitude
2. Bring it to the foot of the cross
3. Actively embrace the spiritual opposite to the sin in question, in the power of the Holy Spirit
4. Renew and refresh your mind and spirit through daily reading and meditating on the Word of God; and develop an active praise life, which will greatly help to counter tendencies to fall into sin.

Perhaps one of the greatest problems for a Christian who is experiencing failure in discipleship through giving way to fleshly desires is confusion regarding the nature of repentance in the Christian life. Repentance (with faith) is not only the means of salvation, and beginning of the Christian life, but is an essential, ongoing necessity for all Christians.

Repentance is not remorse. It is not self-pity, nor is it feeling sorry for the consequences of our sin. It is helpful to realise that there are two kinds of sorrow: godly or worldly sorrow. The distinction can be illustrated as follows: A husband shouts at his wife and fails to spend time with her. He realises he is in the wrong. The Holy Spirit convicts him and prompts him to put it right, which he does by sorting the matter out with her. This is godly sorrow. He might, however, merely regret his behaviour, because he feels embarrassed that the neighbours overheard him! There is no conviction that he has hurt God, but only concern for his own reputation. That is worldly sorrow. If repentance is not remorse or self-pity, neither is it necessarily to do with the intensity of our feelings. Some may cry profusely over their failures, then think that they have repented. Actually, they may just be emotional. Others may feel little, but have truly turned away from the sin in question while thinking they have not repented because they have not felt very much. They may just not be very emotional people. Neither is repentance confession. Many Anglicans think they have repented because every Sunday they join in a prayer of general confession. But that is no evidence of repentance.

Rightly understood, repentance involves a change in heart-attitude towards God. It means realising that our sin has been against God and His love. King David, who committed adultery and organised a murder, recognized that it was, above all, against God that he had sinned:

> Have mercy on me, O God, according to your unfailing love;
> according to your great compassion blot out my transgressions.
> Wash away all my iniquity and cleanse me from my sin.
> For I know my transgressions, and my sin is always

> before me.
> Against you, you only, have I sinned and done what is evil in your sight, so that you are proved right when you speak and justified when you judge.
>
> *Psalm 51:1-4*

Biblical repentance begins with a change of heart towards God. It involves a determination not to hurt God any more and a coming before Him without any excuse at all. David tells Nathan:'I have sinned against the LORD'[2 Samuel 12:13]. Never mind why we did it, the degree of temptation, its apparent irresistibility or the fact that our parents had this fleshly character trait and it therefore seems explicable in us.

True biblical repentance involves saying something like this to the Lord:

> *'I come, Lord, with no excuses, just my sin, for which I am to blame. I ask you to forgive me and make me clean from every stain. Lord Jesus, you suffered in an agony of mind, body and spirit on the cross for that particular sin in my life, and I want to please you by winning the victory in the power of the Spirit in this area of my life. So I turn from this sin and ask for your power to overcome.'*

It can be helpful, literally, to visualise yourself placing the situation at the foot of the cross. As we come to the cross in repentance, the Lord promises to forgive us, and barriers to a close fellowship with Him are removed.

In preparing ourselves for repentance, especially when we are aware of an inner struggle, it may be helpful to remember that repentance is not an unaided human activity, but may be seen as a gift from God, as the following three passages from the New Testament reveal (italics my emphasis):

> The God of our fathers raised Jesus from the dead—whom you had killed by hanging him on a tree. God exalted him to his own right hand as Prince and Saviour that he might *give repentance* and forgiveness of sins to Israel.
>
> *Acts 5:30-31*

> When they heard this, they had no further objections and praised God, saying,"So then, God has *granted even the Gentiles repentance* unto life."
>
> *Acts 11:18*

> And the Lord's servant must not quarrel; instead, he must be kind to everyone, able to teach, not resentful. Those who oppose him he must gently instruct, in the hope that God will *grant them repentance* leading them to a knowledge of the truth....
>
> *2 Timothy 2:24-26*

In each of these passages, repentance is seen as God's gift, and it is therefore entirely appropriate for us to pray, asking Him to give us this gift.

The struggle between the flesh and the Spirit will not be over until the end of the age and the return of Christ. Meanwhile, how we are doing in that struggle will be the most important test of our discipleship—and is, above all, a matter of great concern to our Lord and Saviour Jesus

Christ. As we live more and more in the power of the Holy Spirit, so we will know the wonderful closeness to Jesus that is ours by right as sons and daughters of the living God.

As I learned, when I first struggled with the Lord over the beads of my necklace, one of the most helpful resources in the battle against the flesh is actively to embrace the spiritual opposite of the particular sin that grips me. In the vision of the necklace I 'saw' that compassion is the opposite of jealousy. So, when I am tempted to feel jealous, I am reminded that God wants me to feel compassion in my heart for the person who arouses jealousy within me, and to pray earnestly for blessing on that one's life. Similarly, envy can be countered by consciously praying for the favour of the Lord on the one who is the stumbling block. Fear can be fought off by actively remembering the Lord's faithfulness and promises to me—and standing firm on them. As we call on the Lord's help, pursuing righteousness, we will gain peace of mind, healing in relationships, a growing assurance of God's love for us and His perfect purposes for our lives. We shall also see victories in all sorts of areas where we had formerly known only defeat. This, in turn, leads us to love and praise Him more and more.

Finally, it is by reading the Word of God and meditating on it, and by developing intimacy with Him through prayer and praise, that we can be constantly renewed in our relationship with the Lord Jesus.

> The law of the LORD is perfect,
> reviving the soul.
> The statutes of the LORD are trustworthy,
> making wise the simple.

The precepts of the LORD are right,
giving joy to the heart.
The commands of the LORD are radiant,
giving light to the eyes.
The fear of the LORD is pure,
enduring for ever.
The ordinances of the LORD are sure
and altogether righteous.
They are more precious than gold,
than much pure gold;
they are sweeter than honey,
than honey from the comb.
By them is your servant warned;
in keeping them there is great reward.
Who can discern his errors?
Forgive my hidden faults.
Keep your servant also from wilful sins;
may they not rule over me.
Then will I be blameless,
innocent of great transgression.
May the words of my mouth and the
meditation of my heart
be pleasing in your sight,
O LORD, my Rock and my Redeemer

Psalm 19:7-14